AF834295

Community Conflict Mediation

Fabiana Marion Spengler

Community Conflict Mediation

Springer

Fabiana Marion Spengler
University of Santa Cruz do Sul
Santa Cruz do Sul, Rio Grande do Sul, Brazil

ISBN 978-3-032-09872-6 ISBN 978-3-032-09873-3 (eBook)
https://doi.org/10.1007/978-3-032-09873-3

© The Editor(s) (if applicable) and The Author(s), under exclusive license to Springer Nature Switzerland AG 2025

This work is subject to copyright. All rights are solely and exclusively licensed by the Publisher, whether the whole or part of the material is concerned, specifically the rights of reprinting, reuse of illustrations, recitation, broadcasting, reproduction on microfilms or in any other physical way, and transmission or information storage and retrieval, electronic adaptation, computer software, or by similar or dissimilar methodology now known or hereafter developed.
The use of general descriptive names, registered names, trademarks, service marks, etc. in this publication does not imply, even in the absence of a specific statement, that such names are exempt from the relevant protective laws and regulations and therefore free for general use.
The publisher, the authors and the editors are safe to assume that the advice and information in this book are believed to be true and accurate at the date of publication. Neither the publisher nor the authors or the editors give a warranty, expressed or implied, with respect to the material contained herein or for any errors or omissions that may have been made. The publisher remains neutral with regard to jurisdictional claims in published maps and institutional affiliations.

This Springer imprint is published by the registered company Springer Nature Switzerland AG.
The registered company address is: Gewerbestrasse 11, 6330 Cham, Switzerland

If disposing of this product, please recycle the paper.

Contents

Chapter 1
Introduction

Contemporary society demands a new judicial model in response to the inefficiency of traditional conflict resolution methods. The judicial function, monopolised by the state, no longer provides answers to the conflictuality produced by our complex society, undergoing a crisis of effectiveness (quantitative, but primarily qualitative), which necessitates the search for alternatives. Similarly, the methods and content used by law to respond to disputes do not find adequacy between the complexity of demands, the parties involved, and the legal instruments used. Finally, issues related to the technical-formal character of the language used in judicial rituals and procedures, permeated by bureaucratic aspects, determine the slowness and accumulation of demands.

These observations lead to a loss of confidence in jurisdiction. The proposal, therefore, was to identify community mediation as a means of conflict resolution, proposing a model based on a perspective focused on communication, friendship, otherness, and fraternity. In this way, community mediation emerged as a more suitable resolution to the current conflict complexity. It proposes an "alternative culture", which goes beyond traditional jurisdiction, innovating through consensual and autonomous practices that return to the citizen and the community in which they are inserted (making them responsible) the ability to deal with the litigiousness inherent in their existence.

Community mediation differs from traditional conflict management practices precisely because its workplace is the community—its operations base being the pluralism of values—composed of diverse and alternative life systems. Its purpose is to reopen interrupted communication channels and rebuild destroyed social ties. Its most important challenge is to accept difference and diversity, the dissent and disorder they generate. Its main ambition is not to propose new values, but to re-establish communication between those that each one brings with them.

Taking into account the specificities of community mediation, its political basis was investigated by questioning whether the friendship realised by the Greeks and Romans—as a unifying and reconstructive force of social and political ties—can be considered a foundation for community justice and to what extent this happens.

© The Author(s), under exclusive license to Springer Nature Switzerland AG 2025

F. M. Spengler, *Community Conflict Mediation*,
https://doi.org/10.1007/978-3-032-09873-3_1

In this context, it was important to delimit the *philia* and the *amicitia* of the ancient world and the friendship of modern social systems, considering that the first two cement the city, thus becoming a prerequisite for all political life. The third does not reiterate the community model itself, but separates it, differentiates it, almost immunising itself from the condition of estrangement, if not hostility, that crosses the public sphere.

It is important to note that *amicitia* had, "until the end of the Republic, the function of regulating conflicts by channelling them into peaceful paths, preserving the *status* of the *patria potestas*, as well as establishing links between different families" (Ortega 2002, pp. 47–48). For this to be possible, rules and values were defined within the system of trust (*fides*) and favour (*officium*), which were a fundamental part of virtue (*virtus*) and the dignity (*dignitas*) of the Roman lord. The code of *virtus* imposed a rule of reciprocity, in which each act of friendship should be reciprocated in the future. In these terms, the *amicitia vera* exists only among good men and consists of agreement. The notion of agreement or consensus already evokes a notion of friendship with a strong political and moral basis rather than metaphysical, which adapts to the socio-political reality of Roman society.

In Greek society, on the other hand, friendship performed the functions of social cohesion and protection in a decentralised world, which could not guarantee the lives of individuals, representing a possibility of ensuring existence and the maintenance of society. Comparing the friendship of Greek and Roman societies—especially the fact that they were means of consensus and social cohesion and a reason for community and egalitarian conflict management, without the need to resort to the state—and the friendship of modern social systems, it is observed that the latter is exposed to "risks of interference" and, "when it wins, inserting itself in the public sphere, is ready to transform, at best, into a transversal incident, if not into confusion to be eliminated, in an irrelevant dimension to be set aside thanks to the separation between private and affective life and public life, once it is not identified with familiarity and particularism." (Resta 2020, p. 24). Moreover, it is not uncommon for those in power to choose not the competent, but those who are loyal to them, delegating trust to friendship and perpetuating the mistrust of political struggle. When friendship exposes itself to the risk of trust, it would be reserved only for the sphere of intimacy, delegating investments in relation to institutional trust to the large functional systems (services, technical competencies, etc.) and retracting friendship towards intimacy.

Consequently, the present text aimed to analyse the political foundations of community mediation by scrutinising the motivation that leads a citizen to handle their conflict autonomously and consensually within the community to which they belong, or to direct it to the Judiciary, expecting a decisive ruling from the judge. Thus, the discussion took into account that community mediation operates with the logic of a mediator, a member of the community, who aims to bring a sense of social inclusion to the other residents. Consequently, the debate also turned to the analysis of the main characteristics of this community mediator, including their relationship with the disputants, which can determine the acceptability of their intervention.

In these terms, the central problem of the research proposed the following question: do Roman *amicitia* and Greek *philia* as social "cement" provide a political basis for current community mediation as a means of handling conflicts that enable the empowerment and accountability of the disputants, resulting in autonomous consensus-based decisions? If so, in what terms does this political basis currently reproduce itself?

Linked to this central problem are the other questions: (a) was/is friendship (in Greek and Roman conceptions) considered as a political means of managing social conflicts, based on consensus, alterity, solidarity, and fraternity of the disputants? (b) if the conflicts are addressed by a mediator, who belongs to the same community and shares values, habits, and beliefs with the disputants, will they be handled more appropriately? Among equals, are the chances of autonomy and accountability for dispute resolution real? Can community mediation provide answers to these questions?

To address these research problems, some objectives were outlined. The general objective was: (a) to investigate Roman *amicitia* and Greek *philia* as the political foundation of current community mediation practices, pointing out their main authors. Related to this general objective, other specific objectives were outlined: (a) to define "consensus", "alterity", "fraternity", "solidarity", and "time" as fundamental categories that integrate the concept of friendship and their relations with community mediation and jurisdiction; (b) to identify the limits of community mediation as well as the possibility that its practice results in the autonomy and accountability of the mediators for their choices.

The methodology employed in the research used a deductive approach in which it was intended to start from the investigation of categories considered fundamental for the development of the theme—such as communication, friendship, fraternity, alterity, time, and consensus—to then address the problem itself. The comparative method was used as the procedure method, as it aims to investigate the similarities and differences between jurisdiction and community mediation, as well as the evolution of the latter over time, trying to identify the deficiencies that characterise jurisdiction amidst current conflict complexity. The research technique applied was bibliographic research based on indirect documentation that served as a theoretical basis for the development of the study.

However, before the debate led to community mediation, it delved into the concept of current and ancient friendship, visiting the main authors who discuss Greek and Roman friendship. Subsequently, the text addressed fraternity and the political game of friend/enemy. The time of the process and the time of mediation were the next approach, with all their differences.

Finally, the community mediation model was dissected as a means of generating autonomy. In this context, friendship was debated as a bond enabling direct communication, building a conflict management strategy based on a legal matrix that relates to historical subjects and not just procedural subjects; that allows surpassing the triadic barrier (judge, plaintiff, and defendant), allowing the conflict to be seen as a physiological "treatable" event, but not always "solvable"; that enables a quantitative leap in the treatment of current conflictuality through the establishment of a new culture that goes beyond the positivist dichotomy of winner/loser to revisit the possibility of gain for both parties, sharing a state of being "with" the other and not "against" the other, making the community space not the moment of the "deciding judge", but of the mutually consensual, autonomous, and accountable "parties".

References

Books

Ortega, F (2002) Genealogias da Amizade. Coleção Políticas de Imanência. Iluminuras, São Paulo
Resta, E (2020) O Direito Fraterno. Essere nel Mondo, Santa Cruz do Sul

Chapter 2
Between *Philia*, *Amicitia* and Friendship: Social Cement or Legal Rule?

Friendship has been celebrated in prose and verse, it has given rise to tales, texts and legends. Always permeated by other feelings such as loyalty and trust, friendship is a strong relationship that is not born and does not persist through blood ties or kinship. In fact, it is the "least natural" of the emotional bonds that a human being possesses: the least instinctive, less organic, biological and gregarious, yet it is the most indispensable. The bond of friendship is not the result of a need nor an organic determination: it is born from preference and choice.

Perhaps because friendship is such a special bond, the word "friend" is not defined with precision even by the dictionary. Perhaps the dictionary can explain what a friend is in the semantic sense of the term, but it cannot give this explanation the emotional importance it possesses. Thus, a friend is defined as a person with whom there is a bond based on affection and esteem; it is the preferred companion linked to the other by a feeling of mutual affection and intimacy; following this conception, a friend is precisely the opposite of an enemy.

Despite the importance that friendship assumes in the organisation, maintenance and cohesion of social groups, there are no detailed histories of the bonds generated from it in any great civilization, western or eastern. Despite knowing texts that reflect great friendships like that between Montaigne and Étienne de La Boétie (La Boétie 1999), it refers to a complex and disordered feeling which makes its exact delimitation difficult.

However, even if disordered, friendship has been used, politically, as a pact or contract that goes beyond emotional limits and serves as a means of maintaining social alliances established. This security regarding the pact is given especially due to feelings related to it such as loyalty, trust and gratitude.

However, here we are talking about a loyalty, a trust and a gratitude that are not standardised or legalised, that are not even mentioned because they compose the world of feelings and not the world of justice. All this because, according to Aristotle (2005, p. 4), where there is friendship we do not need justice. Where friendship prevails, good faith and trust do not need to be legally guaranteed. They

© The Author(s), under exclusive license to Springer Nature Switzerland AG 2025
F. M. Spengler, *Community Conflict Mediation*,
https://doi.org/10.1007/978-3-032-09873-3_2

are part of a context lived and experienced by friends. If friendship ceases to be mortar, social cement, then we need the guarantees of Law.

In this sense, this chapter aimed to investigate the *amicitia* of the Romans and the *philia* of the Greeks as the political foundation of current community mediation practices, highlighting their main authors. This is due to the fact that community mediation works with a paradigm that dispenses with the figure of the judge—a third party who dictates the Law—, to be based on the figure of the mediator—a person who helps people to communicate in a more appropriate way—.

In this way, community mediation works with the trust and friendship placed in the mediator and the other conflicting party without the need for codified rules for conflict resolution. To reach this point of the debate, this chapter first investigated friendship broadly before delving into the detailed debate of Greek *philia* and *amiticia* using their main authors: Aristotle, Plato and Cicero.

Finally, friendship and its political aspects were visited interweaving its historical connotation with other categories such as justice and trust.

2.1 From Genesis to Fragmentation: The Privatisation of the Public Relationship of Friendship and Its Maintenance Under the Yoke of the State

It is no coincidence that Cicero (2001, p. 24) begins his text entitled "On Friendship" stating "I can only exhort you to put friendship before all human things, for there is nothing that conforms so much to our nature, nor is more suitable for happiness or misfortune".

The fact is that the word friendship is difficult to define because it does not have a single meaning, but several. This reality has been present since the Greek and Roman civilizations. Two thousand years ago Aristotle (2005) was already agonising and writing about the distinction between types of friendship aiming to identify, among them, the one that was "true".

Thus, what is perceived is that although the core of friendship—expressed by La Boètie (1999, p. 206), among many others—is kindness,

While the essence of friendship—its naturalness and reciprocity—remains the same, its appearance is protean, potentially blending with that which imitates and denies it. After all, even among pirates, there is some faith in the sharing of plunder because they are equals and comrades.

At first glance, friendship seems to be confined to the moment when nature, operating alone, creates and preserves companions in a kind of natural sociability. When this process ends with the advent of political society, only a few remain who remember the previous instant, as if, in the present, friendship were merely a memory of what preceded the denaturalisation. Under the influence of the necessary illusions that preside over the division of will and the creation and maintenance of society, it seems to change in form (confused with flattery and complicity), quality (from natural to cultivated), quantity (from all, only a few remain), time (from present to memory), and place (from the centre of sociability to the periphery). (La Boétie 1999, p. 206).

But if friendship is so difficult to define and has this polymorphic aspect, what can one then expect from a friend? That they share the image I have of myself or, at least, that they do not deviate too far from it? Yes, because if it is too favourable, it gives the impression of flattery. If it is too negative, it can bring a sense of injustice, contradicting a basic requirement of friendship. In this sense, friends should have similar reciprocal images. Not identical, of course, because then there would be nothing to discover, but without excessive dissonances.

For a long time, humanity lived with solid friendship relations, with close and enduring ties, in the real sense of the term. During this period, laws and rules about the organisation and maintenance of social ties were not codified (because it was unnecessary). Friendship was the cement that united and strengthened these relationships. It was maintained through a binary code divided between friend/enemy, which was sufficient to point out the relationships that should be protected and those that were repulsive.

Currently, we see the persistence of the political game that involves the binary code friend/enemy. However, friendship has lost its capacity for cohesion and strengthening of social ties and has been replaced by codified laws and rules.[1]

In this vein, friendship distances itself from the public sphere (organisation and social cohesion, sense of belonging) and approaches the private sphere (kinship and blood ties, ties inherent to work and leisure relationships). However, in both spheres, state intervention is relied upon for their maintenance and even in the resolution of conflicts arising from them (if they have a legal, codified bias). The fact is that we have lost friends in the true, legitimate sense of the term and gained acquaintances or companions. We live with them in a harmonious or conflictual way, all under the relentless eye of the State that establishes and applies the rules determining our public and private relations.

The importance of true friendship relationships has been lost. Nowadays, even when people refer to a friend, they no longer do so in the Greek or Roman sense of the term. Thus, contemporarily "friends are also strangers, unseen, not neighbouring", in this way "they evade the bond of daily reciprocity, built from a common air that is breathed. One can share life without sharing it" (Resta 2020, p. 18).

The driving force behind this process of particularisation of friendship occurs with the familiarisation[2] of society and the consequent emptying of public space.[3] In this interim, the fate of friendship culminates in the absorption of all forms of

[1] The same happened with trust, which became juridified and divided into good and bad faith.

[2] This movement of transformation of family ties will not be the object of analysis in the present research due to space and time constraints. On the subject, it is important to read Elias, Norbert. *The Court Society* (2001); Elias, Norbert. *The Civilising Process* (1994) and Arendt, Hannah. *The Human Condition* (2004).

[3] It is no longer the "public" that tends to colonise the "private". What happens is the opposite: it is the private that colonises the public space, squeezing and expelling whatever cannot be fully

sociability into the family structure. Thus, the process of "disappearance of public sociability, of emptying of public space, corresponds to the emergence of the modern family, which monopolised other forms of sociability" (Ortega 2002, p. 107). Consequently, according to Francisco de Ortega, this process, combined with other factors such as the emergence of the category of "homosexuals", the conjugalisation of love, and the incorporation of sexuality into marriage, constituted the main determinants of the decline of friendship practices in the nineteenth century (Ortega 2002, p. 107).

According to the author (Ortega 2002, p. 107), three fundamental factors would have conditioned the process of privatisation and impoverishment of the relational fabric of Western societies:

(a) the fact that the State began to play a new role from the fifteenth century, intervening increasingly frequently in the social space previously left to communities. The process of formation of modern states and centralisation of society, which correlates with the reorganisation and historical change of psychic economy, point in the same direction by underlining the decisive role played by the State in shaping private life and sociability, which follows a path of increasing privatisation and intimacy. As a main consequence, from this movement, the State progressively began to interfere and manage the lives of individuals more directly;
(b) a second important factor in this process was the development of literacy, as well as the spread of reading facilitated by the invention of the press, which allows for solitary reflection; solitude itself will change its *status*, no longer being associated with boredom and starting to develop, from the seventeenth century onwards, a taste for solitary retreat;
(c) finally, new forms of religion allowed the development of private devotion and solitary meditation. Obviously, this process of privatisation in Western societies since the sixteenth and seventeenth centuries has conditioned forms of sociability and friendship in particular.

In Greece, as we will see later, the *philia* was placed above the family, it was linked to the public space, to action in freedom, to politics. The Christian fraternal tradition probably historically contributed to this primacy of family images over those of friendship. Similarly, the Roman ideal of trust and loyalty to a friend, the *fides*, transformed into total trust in God. Therefore, Christianity replaced the intimacy of friends with a bond of love and charity that embraces all without restriction. As a result, there is an expansion of friendship and its political emptiness. The friendship that previously turned to the *polis* is now charity (*caritas*), directed towards divine love and to paradise.

The *caritas* signifies love for one's neighbour and a totality, a broad community love, detached from the singularity and particularity of a love "for

expressed, without leaving residues, in the vernacular of care, anxieties and private initiatives (Bauman 2001, p. 49).

two". Therefore, it is concluded that the *Amicitia* is not *agape,* and this substitution leads to the depersonalisation of such feeling making it charitable, but without affection. Christian friendship as perfect friendship is the one that makes lived friendships, those real ones, without qualities. It is inherent to Christianity the replacement of friendship by agape, considered a form of perfect friendship.

This outlines the ambivalence between friendship and love in Christianity. Friendship became a suspicious relationship and love (to God and to the neighbour) was the means of liberation. Just like the *amicitia* of the Romans, the *philia* of the Greeks is also rejected for its selfish and instrumental character, while the *agape* represents true friendship, as it does not manifest an interpersonal attraction. In other words, the friend should no longer be loved for himself, but for God. The *philia* thus becomes *caritas christiana*, the love of God that unites all men. *Caritas* constitutes the essence of friendship in Christianity (Ortega 2002, p. 73).

It is possible to perceive, thus, how the conceptions of friendship relations as belonging to intimacy, disconnected and distanced from the public, and often incorporated into kinship relations—which currently seems natural and unquestionable—are, in reality, a recent phenomenon, initiated in the nineteenth century.

This new way of seeing friendship—now known and recognised as fraternity, wrapped in divine love—includes because it excludes, neighbours because it distances, rebuilds vital tissues while destroying others; it seems, like love, a normal improbability. This is the great divide between the *philia* of the ancient world and the friendship of modern social systems; while the former is what cements the city, being, therefore, a prerequisite for any political life that generalises the private, reproducing it in public life, the latter does not reiterate its own community model, but separates it, differentiates it from it almost immunising itself from the condition of estrangement, if not of enmity, that crosses the public sphere. Therefore, it is exposed to the risks of interference and, when it wins, inserting itself into the public sphere, it is ready to transform itself, at best, into a transversal incident, if not into confusion to be eliminated, into an irrelevant dimension to be set aside due to the separation between private and affective life and public life, when, even, it is not identified with familiarity and particularity; moreover, it is not uncommon for those in power to choose not the competent, but those who are loyal to them, delegating trust to friendship and perpetuating the distrust of political struggle (Resta 2020, pp. 24–25).

This trajectory paves the way in modernity through a clear separation, unthinkable in the ancient world, between friendship and love. Against the risk of an overly personal and, therefore, selfish expansion of friendship, generalised *charitas* was recommended which imposes to love God in each of the other men. While worldly friendship leaves room for the quality of individuals ("because you are you"), charitable friendship is foreign to it and chooses impersonality. (Resta 2020, p. 25)

On this path, and continuing the debate that compares *philia* of the Greeks, *amicitia* of the Romans and modern friendship (fraternity) the following item will investigate the *philia* Greek.

2.2 Greek Philia as a Character Disposition that Desires the Good of the Other

The Greek concept and delimitation of *philia* appears in Herodotus in the fifth century BC. However, *Phílos* (a word descendant from *philia)* was used by Homer with a possessive (predominant) and affective sense. In the possessive sense, *phílos* does not refer to a friendship, but rather constitutes a mark of possession without reference to a person, referring to: "yours" or "mine", it could also designate animals, objects or body parts, etc. (Ortega 2002, p. 17)

In the affective sense, *philos* is an expression of close or kinship relations. "The meaning of the verb *philein* is also ambiguous, designating the action of influence over people who are protected: women, children, relatives, slaves. *Philein* also has the sense of expressing hospitality, of receiving foreigners, and of kissing, as a sign of recognition among the *phíloi*, as appears in Herodotus referring to the behaviour among the Persians" (Ortega 2002, pp. 17–18).

It is important to note that *philia* was a philosophical theme widely discussed in classical antiquity. The social structure of Greece at that time reserved a very special "place" for friendship, which, today unfortunately no longer exists, at least not with that personal meaning and ethical-political intensity (Schaefer 2010, p. 19).

In classical Greece, friendship and hospitality (*xenia*) are very close relations to the point of defining friends and foreigners. The institution of *xenia* is a way of relating to the foreigner, through a long-distance bond that includes reciprocal obligations and benefits. Compared to the bond of the *philói*, *xenia* differed because it was a relationship at a distance. This fact implied the physical separation of the participants, as well as its broad political reach, as these aristocratic networks extended beyond cities and even the Greek world. Thus, the institution of *xenia* had and fulfilled a defined "political-strategic function: the communities of the time were in a situation of distrust and hostility among them, of "armed peace", *xenia* was a way to guarantee protection, support and armament to the foreigner". From the moment the *polis* were formed, the networks of *xenias* continued to exist, which contributed to the maintenance of a strong component of ritualisation and institutionalisation in the predominant affective relations in the *polis* (Ortega 2002, p. 22).

In addition to *philia*, ancient Greece also had another kind of association between friends called *heteria* which was the political relationship of military camaraderie, a kind of fraternity in arms or a "political club", in which men of the same age and social class joined in youth and stayed until old age. The *heteria* constituted an indispensable element of political life in the *polis,* a relationship that was articulated as a bond of friendship. In addition, it horizontally crossed the basic kinship structures, linking and unifying the different power centres. The *heteria* represented a strong affective bond, an "expressive friendship". Precisely for this reason, it was one of the strongest and most persistent social institutions in the Greek world, which managed to maintain itself through numerous changes of government and revolutions (Ortega 2002, pp. 22–23).

Thus, in Homeric Greece, friendship does not appear defined in a clear and unique way, with numerous types and notions existing. Many friendship relations were institutionalised relations that left little room for freedom of choice, spontaneity and personal preferences. This type of friendship performed the functions of social cohesion and protection in a decentralised world, which could not guarantee the life of individuals, representing a possibility to ensure the existence and maintenance of society (Ortega 2002, pp. 22–23).[4]

However, with the evolution of the concept of *philia,* kinship relations linked to friendship weakened until they completely dissociated. Friendship began to be defined by its character of free choice and personal affection, becoming an independent institution. The main consequence for interpersonal relations was the separation of these from institutionalised relations. However, this did not occur in relation to *philia*. This maintained, throughout the classical Greek era, a strong institutionalised and ritualised dimension.

In this way, it was possible to observe that affective relations were established normatively and the tasks of friendship were institutionalised. This happened because in the *polis* of Greece, friendship relations played a considerable role, but there was a supplementary institutional framework that implied a system of obligations, duties and reciprocal tasks, the establishment of a hierarchy among friends, etc. Friendship relations formed the atoms of the *polis*, the condition of its survival (Ortega 2002, p. 24).

In this context, Plato[5] debates friendship as the basis for the search for truth, a characteristic of philosophy. In Lysis, the dialogue highlights the idea that friendship implies a communion of material and spiritual goods, thus becoming a useful thing. It also emphasises that there is a distinction between "the one who loves" and "the one who is loved". From this debate also creates the difference between the friend and the enemy.

In fact, before defining the concept of *philia*, "friendship", it is necessary to concretely define what *philos*, "friend", an ambiguous term that implies, for example, the distinction between lover, the one who feels love or friendship, in which, let's say, the desire to possess the object of his love begins, and loved. We can use, respectively for each one, the expressions active term and passive term. Thus, Plato states: "a friend is not the one who loves, but the one who is loved" (Plato 1995, p. 47).

---

[4] Perhaps this was the main human loss when we talk about friendship that ceased to be social cement and perhaps this is a great reconquest: to return to man the ability to find and maintain friendships that can perform these functions of cohesion and protection making less important and necessary the performance of these functions by state institutions (for example, the Judiciary).

[5] It is important to say that the basis for the debate started here were Plato's dialogues in which the philosopher addresses *philia* directly: in *Lysis,* in *Symposium* and in *Phaedrus.* The first of them (*Lysis*) was the one that centralised the interest of this text. This is because, despite the aporetic character of the text, it is, however, the one that comes closest to the definition of the concept of friendship.

In Plato's work, there is a strong erotic connotation in the analysis of friendship. This is due to the "absence of strong marital bonds and conjugal love, as well as the strict separation of the sexes—designating specific places for each one—, led the classical *polis* to concentrate passion and tenderness in relations between men" (Ortega 2002, p. 25). Thus, the privilege of the cult of friendship and male love is seen.

As little importance was attributed to the female sex (women were removed from the public sphere, relegated to the domestic space), male relations (between men) were marked by affection and emotional significance. In this way, the disciples, traditionally beautiful boys, were the substitutes for women because they physically resembled them, being considered objects of desire.

Thus, friendship relations (which necessarily established between men, as women were considered incapable of maintaining them) were eroticised relations. Such relationships presupposed the freedom of the individuals involved, which was visibly expressed in the game of seduction, in the possibility of saying "no" and in the refusal of courtship. Only free men could be recipients of this erotic relationship. Heterosexual relations were strongly codified, belonged to marriage or brothels and remained prohibited outside this regulation. The female role in this context was to accept male desires, as women depended on them economically, satisfying their sexuality, ensuring procreation and administration of the estate.

However, Francisco de Ortega (2002, p. 29 and following) points out that there was a difficulty in the Greek morality of *eros,* originated from the isomorphism existing in Hellenic society between sexual relations and social behaviour, which prevented the boy, with passive behaviour in the sexual relationship, as an object of pleasure of the older man, from being able to perform an active role as a citizen of the *polis*. Thus, the "antinomy of the boys" consisted in being considered as objects of pleasure, and yet, they could not identify with this status as future citizens, since only women and slaves were objects of pleasure.

Consequently, the Platonic reflection of *philia* emerges as an attempt to respond to this antinomy, that is, as a possibility of endowing *eros* with a morally accepted form (Plato 1995). In this sense, the strategy consisted in transforming *eros* into the relationship of *philia*, excluding the sexual element (sublimated), which allows him to maintain the "pedagogical" elements of boy's love, without falling into the antinomies implied in traditional erotica.

Finally, Ortega (2002) concludes that Plato (1995) was not very interested in distinguishing between love and friendship in the dialogues that deal with the subject, as it is precisely from this conceptual fluidity that the important shifts originate that will lead to friendship as a kind of sublimated *eros*.

Following the same line of reasoning, Aristotle (2005) completely dissociates the notion of erotic love from the notion of *philia*, creating a definitive incompatibility between them. This Aristotelian notion will remain constant in the history of friendship.

Thus, from Aristotelian reasoning, friendship excludes itself from Platonic passivity, becoming an activity, the very philosophical activity; love, on the other hand, is considered a non-philosophical impulse. Thus, it is possible to summarise by saying that Eros is a passion and *philia* an *ethos*, love begins to be seen as an emotion; friendship, in turn, is interpreted as a disposition of character.

According to the Aristotelian construction, *philia* is characterised by habit, expressing itself as a moral and intellectual attitude with the main objective of reciprocal love between friends, whose basis is the freedom of will and choice in which each one wishes good for the other (Aristotle 1996, p. 257). With his dissociation of *eros* and *philia*, Aristotle (1996, p. 257) intended to remove the possibility of this "misuse" of *eros*.

For Aristotle, people are friends for three main reasons: for the utility they seek, for the pleasure they expect, and for the good that individuals wish for each other. Thus, the philosopher emphasises that: "friends whose affection is based on interest do not love each other for themselves, but because of some benefit they get from each other" (Aristotle 1996, p. 259). The same applies when the basis of the relationship is the pleasure obtained.

Thus, he states that such friendships are merely accidental, as it is not for being who she is that the person is loved, but for providing some benefit or pleasure to the other. Such friendships easily dissolve if the people do not remain as they were initially, for if one of them is no longer pleasant or useful the other ceases to love her. And utility is not a permanent quality, but is always changing. Therefore, once the reason for the friendship disappears, it dissolves, as it exists only as a means to an end (Aristotle 1996, pp. 259–260).

Consequently, the first two forms of friendship are perishable and circumstantial, that is, they are not referred to the essence of a true friendship.

However, the third form of friendship is characterised by wishing good for the other. Perfect friendship exists between good people and those similar in terms of moral excellence; in this case, each of the people wishes well for the other in an identical way, because the other person is good, and they are good in themselves.

In this line of reasoning, Aristotle (1996) points out happiness, virtue and friendship as linked categories. This is especially the case when the friend is seen as a "second self" or an "other self". At the base of love for the friend is self-love. Thus, Aristotle (1996) states that self-awareness, personal identity, is given by the other, in the contemplation of the other, as our mirror image. In friendship, the individual becomes another, leaves himself, objectifies himself; it is necessary to become aware of the other's thought and activity to be aware of one's own thought and activity, a condition of *eudaimonia*. Self-awareness is preceded by awareness of the other, the perception of the friend is the privileged form of perception and self-awareness (Ortega 2002, pp. 41–42).

It is in this sense that Ortega shows that this notion of self-awareness via awareness of another constitutes a notion of subjectivity different from ours. To construct this statement, the author cites Vernant (1989, pp. 215–216) whose texts demonstrate how, for the Greeks, the "I" was neither delimited nor unified, constituting an "open field of forces". Thus, the individual projects and objectifies himself in the activities and works he carries out and which allow him to apprehend himself; it is an outward-facing experience, the individual finds and apprehends himself in others.[6] This is because the Greeks were unaware of introspection. The subject is extroverted; self-awareness is not "reflective", but "existential". Consciousness is outward-facing; self-consciousness, in the modern sense of the term, does not exist, or only in the form of a "he" and not an "I" (Ortega 2002, p. 42).

However, to delimit the genesis and transformations of friendship over time, it is necessary to investigate *Roman amicitia.* outlining its similarities and differences with the *Greek philia.* This, therefore, is the topic that will be developed further.

2.3 The Individual Will of Friends Subordinated to the Rules of the State in *Roman Amicitia*

Roman society had manifestations of friendship seemingly in the same way and very similar to those found in Greek society. It is possible to verify that the Latin terms *amicitia* (friendship), *amicus* (friend), *amare* (to love) seem to correspond to the Greek terms, *philia, philos, philein.* However, despite such similarities, there are important differences. The *Roman amicitia* is a relationship based on free affection, excluding economic associations, religious and legal communities, and kinship relations. Political associations existing between nobles with the aim of mutual support in internal and external political matters and in public office elections were considered forms of *Roman amicitia.* Moreover, and primarily, the *Roman amicitia* is a concept of foreign policy, constituted by mutual exchanges.

Due to this importance acquired by the *amicitia,* the "influence and personal relations of the head of the family were indispensable for success in politics". This was because the horizontal extensions of the heads of families were constituted by the relations of *amicitia,* alliances with people of the same class and *social status* (Ortega 2002, pp. 47–48). Similarly, the *amicitia* and *patrocinium* relations were not formed by groups of the same age, so they did not present the degree of conviviality and emotional involvement of the Greek *heterias,* not to mention the loss of pedagogical meaning of the *eros paidikon.* These functions were performed in Roman society by the family (Ortega 2002, p. 48).

Consequently, Roman friendship did not have the same importance as Greek friendship. This statement is true in all senses: cultural, erotic, and emotional. For the Romans, there was no mix/relationship between *eros* and *philia.* The Romans confined *eros* to the conjugal bond.[7]

---

[6] The relationship with the other, which was named "alterity" in this research, will be addressed in the next chapter. On the subject, it is important to read Lévinas, Emmanuel. *Between us: essays on alterity.*

[7] On the subject, it is important to consider Foucault's construction that points to a "new/other erotic", replacing the Greek erotic of boys. This erotic is based on and presents marriage as a way of life, relegating *Eros* to the conjugal bond. This new erotic reality is constituted around the reciprocal and symmetrical relationship of man and woman, pointing to virginity as a growing value, as a lifestyle and a higher form of existence, and the perfect union they aim to achieve (Foucault 2004, 2005).

This change in customs occurs especially with the end of the *polis,* a moment in which pederasty loses its pedagogical and military function (inheritance from the Hellenic world) and its philosophical foundation, becoming in the eyes of all, a despicable perversion. The rules of the Roman Republic, which valued the family as a moral and not just economic institution, condemned and viewed homosexuality with repugnance.

Noble families dominated Roman public life. The Romans recognised three ways to achieve glory: the family, money, and personal relations, in which the *amicitia* is the most important, along with the relations of *patrocinium.* Thus, the success of a politician was determined according to the number and importance of his clients and friends. Under these circumstances, the *amicitia* became a strictly utilitarian and self-interested relationship, aiming to achieve reciprocal advantages. In these relations, ethical and emotional motivations were replaced by practical considerations, in which hypocrisy, selfishness, and pretence took the place of trust and honesty (Ortega 2002, p. 50).

In Rome, according to Ortega (2002, pp. 50–51), the distance between the philosophical discourse on *amicitia* and the social practice of friendship is greater than in Greece, where the philosophical theory of *philia*—especially with Aristotle (1996) who aimed for a phenomenological description, a typology of the forms of *philia* in the *polis*—was in correlation with the practice of friendship in Hellenic society. Along the same lines, the author points out that it is possible to find in Cicero (2001) the first discourse on friendship, in which the distance between theoretical reflection and social practice is almost immeasurable. From now on, the great discourses on *philia/amicitia* are personalised discourses (funeral discourses of mourning for the loss of a friend, as we find in Cicero, Augustine, and Montaigne, among others), there being an insurmountable abyss between them and the social practice of friendship, which leads to the hyperbolisation of the utopian-idealist character of these discourses.

Thus, despite the character of "mutual benefit" of Roman friendship, With its consequent remnants of obligation for the compliance with rules and for the maintenance of social peace, it had, until the end of the Republic, the function of regulating conflicts by channelling them into peaceful paths. Fulfilling this mission, the *amicitia* preserved the *status* of the *patria potestas*, as well as established links between different families. To achieve this aim, rules and values were defined within the system of trust (*fides*) and favour (*officium*), a fundamental part of virtue (*virtus*) and the dignity (*dignitas*) of the Roman lord. The code of *virtus* imposed a rule of reciprocity, in which each act of friendship should be reciprocated in the future (Ortega 2002, p. 51).

Thus, at the base of the Ciceronian theory of friendship, one will find concord, highlighting the Greek *philia* as the foundation of the State. Concord would thus constitute the harmony resulting from rivalry, whose main function of regulation and facilitation was attributed to *Amicitia*. However, if concord turns into discord, as will happen at the end of the Republic, *amicitia* no longer serves as a pacifying instance, becoming a source of conspiracy. It is in this context that Cicero's theory of *amicitia* should be situated (Ortega 2002, p. 51).

For Cicero, the types of friendship are divided in the same way as in Aristotle. Thus, also in the Ciceronian theory, pleasure and utility appear as the primary cause of friendship. On a secondary level, as an ideal and perfect relationship comes the *amicitia vera*, or *amicitia perfecta*, which corresponds to the Aristotelian *teleia philia*. In this sense, Cicero emphasizes that "only among the good can there be friendship". And he adds: "I do not exaggerate in this, as do those who deal with such issues with subtlety, perhaps true, but little useful for the good of all: they deny, in fact, that a man can be good if he is not wise. Let it be so, but they consider a wisdom that no mortal can achieve" (Cicero 1993, n.p.).

Following this line of reasoning, Cicero asserts that the *Amicitia vera* exists only among good men and can be defined as "the perfect agreement of all divine and human things, accompanied by benevolence and affection, and I believe that, except for wisdom, men have received nothing better from the gods" (Cicero 1993, n.p.). This "perfect agreement" is nothing more than the *consensio*. The notion of *consensio*, agreement or consensus, is important for the present debate, as it already evokes a notion of friendship with a strong political and moral foundation rather than metaphysical, which adapts to the socio-political reality of Roman society.[8] This friendship is only possible among "good men" [...]; he adds that he is not referring to the wise as the Stoics did, but to good men in the sense of concrete experience in Roman society, possessors of a political-practical wisdom linked to responsibility in the State. That is, men recognized as virtuous (*virtus*) in Roman society (Ortega 2002, pp. 51–52).

Ortega goes further by emphasizing that the foundation of Roman friendship lies in the *virtus* of the partners, which, however, has a different character from the Greek virtue (*arete*), manifesting itself in the attainment of personal excellence and glory for the performance of great actions in the service of the Roman State. The Roman noble practices great actions for the Republic, which recognizes him publicly and eternally for his *gloria*. The civil virtue, at the base of the Ciceronian notion of *amicitia*, subordinates the individual will of friends to the interests of the State.

The Roman notion of virtue, very well expressed in Cicero's texts, leads him to place the State, the *patria*, above friendship. This statement can be corroborated by observing the issue of conflict between duties to the State and to the friend, an introductory theme of the limits of friendship (Cicero 2004). Unlike the Greek philosophers who placed duties to the friend above duties to the *polis* (this is given by the analysis and verification of the superior position enjoyed by *philia* in relation to justice), Cicero defends duties to the State as being superior to duties to the friend. His notion of *virtus* and of good implies agreeing with the State: it is immoral, "dishonourable", to support a *amicus contra patriam*, the Ciceronian law of friendship demands that friends do what is "honourable" (*honesto*) (Cicero 1993, n.p). This translates, according to his ideal of virtue, into performing great deeds for the State. A *vir bonus* would never oppose the *res publica* (Ortega 2002, pp. 52–53).

---

[8] This topic will be revisited in Chapter IV when the consensus obtained from mediated communication will be investigated.

Consequently, one can see in the *amicitia* of Rome the preponderance of the interests of the State over the interests of friends, which in itself differentiates this from the Greek *philia*. In this sense, it is possible to affirm that this was perhaps the first change in friendship relations: the concept of "other" is subordinate to the concept of the State. Friendship begins to lose ground, and its ethical principle is gradually replaced by the guarantees offered by codified law. This topic will be addressed in the next section.

2.4 The Relations Between *Philia, Amicitia*, Trust and Justice: From Moral to Legal

In this context, it should not be overlooked that throughout all of Greek antiquity, as was highlighted, there was a close link between friendship and justice underpinning the configuration of *philia* as a political phenomenon. In archaic Greece, it is possible to find a notion of justice (*dike*) characteristic of an aristocratic society, which could be translated as helping/benefiting friends and harming enemies. This form of justice was regulated and administered by the *hetairoi.*[9]

However, with the transition to the classical era and the emergence of democracy, both justice and friendship underwent transformations and were redefined. From this point on, feelings of friendship, the equality of rights and the community of justice existing in small groups constituted as *heterias*, are shifted to the society (*demos*) as a whole. As a consequence, each citizen becomes a friend and equality (*isonomia*), restricted until this time to the *heterias*, belongs to the entire body of citizens.

Thus, in the transition from the old notion of justice to the new (described by Plato as harmony and proportion in the soul and in the *polis*), the notion of friendship provided the element of equality of rights (*isonomia*). With this, friendship is co-extensive with citizenship, and all citizens are, in principle, friends among themselves. Or brothers? For, Aristotle establishes, as we have seen, a proximity between fraternity and comradeship (*heteria*) on one hand, and between fraternity and democracy on the other. The friendship between brothers is close to comradeship precisely because of equality. Political equality is equality among brothers (Ortega 2002, pp. 53–54).

In this sense, Aristotle (1996) asserted that true friends have no need for justice. But what does he mean by this? From the analysis of the text, it can be inferred that Aristotle's statement refers to the fact that the virtue of justice exists to resolve differences between men. Thus, life in the *polis* opens up a series of differential

[9] The *hetairoi* constituted the elite cavalry of Alexander the Great's army. They were formed by squadrons of 200 to 300 soldiers and were known for their interesting and well-organised war strategies.

possibilities: differences in behaviours, ideas, regarding property or the distribution of goods, ethnic differences, etc.

In these cases, it is necessary to resolve differences/conflicts and justice can be invoked as a virtue of the mean, that is, possibility of balancing the differences between excess and deficiency. Thus, recourse to justice occurs as a means of recognising differences or disproportionality.

However, true friendship is not constituted by differences but by similarities. The similarity between individuals considered true friends is the goodness of both. Of course, there can be individuals with different concrete goodness, just as there are many different concrete triangles. This, however, does not shake the similarity that characterises will or triangularity. Both one attribute and the other are what they are, as they are established by what is common in the midst of differences—goodness or triangularity. Goodness does not present itself as either excess or deficiency and is also not a mean. For this reason, certainly, goodness does not lie in the field of justice (Schaefer 2010).

Without a shadow of a doubt, there is a relationship between friendship and justice, since both occur between the same things, refer to the same people, and increase and decrease in the same proportion.

The same applies to friendship and politics. Considering that in Aristotle (1996) the objective of politics is "to produce friendship", it is possible to observe the existence of a fundamental relationship between friendship and politics, also expressed in the concept of civil friendship (*politike philia*), which would unite all citizens of the *polis*. Thus, according to Aristotle (1996), the familial model and, consequently, the pre-political model provides the basis, the foundation, the origin, the structure and the form to political and friendship relations. The family, the *oikos*, however, belongs to the private sphere, which is governed by necessity and violence, in parallel to the political sphere, to the public world as a space of freedom, contingency, action. The same movement that politicises friendship, by linking it to justice and politics, depoliticises it, by linking it to the pre-political structures of the family (Ortega 2002, p. 44).

This Aristotelian logic that links friendship and politics is also used to address friendship in fraternal relations, since it is based on the consecration of friendship to democracy. In these terms, the *politeía* is a matter of brothers (*tôn adelphôn*), but fraternity is not political, when it adopts as a condition the suppression of differences and plurality (considering all individuals as equal), because in these cases the conditions of the political are nullified. On the other hand, friendship is more oriented towards the world and therefore is considered a political phenomenon.

The Aristotelian logic brings the friendship between brothers closer to the aforementioned relations of camaraderie (*heteria*). This is because these relations of *heteria* have great chances of developing among brothers, since they are equal, usually in the same age group, and are similar in their feelings and character. Thus, there is a relationship in the *polis* between politics-friendship-democracy-fraternity-camaraderie, which in a presumed repoliticisation of friendship, would depoliticise it (Ortega 2002, p. 46).

On the other hand, in Epicureanism, friendship represents a withdrawal from politics. Friendship develops in an individual context and constitutes more as a moral phenomenon than a political one. The loss of the political meaning of *philia* is a result of the decrease in the importance of the *polis*. The idea of friendship as a political phenomenon can only be possible in a world where the political action of individuals is effective, which was not the case in the Hellenistic period, with the transition from the *polis* to the empire (Ortega 2002, p. 54).

In Roman society, the *amicitia* ceases to be the social bond par excellence and begins to designate a type of social relationship among others. Thus, the place of *philia* is occupied by consensus, the basic political bond. Politics is no longer based on friendship and even, in some relationships and at certain times, it can be its antithesis. Consensus makes possible the existence of *amicitia* and the exercise of virtue; without consensus, friendship can only exist as a withdrawal from politics.

This is because friendship relations become a means of achieving glory, which makes *amicitia* a utilitarian relationship. From this moment, all ethical and emotional considerations involved in it are relegated to a secondary level in the face of the possible practical advantages that can be derived from the relationship.

However, it is necessary to create mechanisms such as trust (the *fides*) to ensure the fulfilment of obligations arising from the relationship with a minimum of honesty. In this sense, Resta (2009, pp. 52–53) demonstrates how this rupture occurs in the Aristotelian text, pinpointing the exact point at which friendship loses its importance in structuring relations, necessitating the use of other categories, among them and primarily trust (*fiducia*). Thus:

> Un noto testo di Aristotele, tratto dall'*Etica nicomachea* (1162b, 20-35), ci mostra meglio di qualsiasi saggio di teoria sociale il gioco della fiducia e ci aiuta a disverlarne la patina di opacità. Aristotele racconta di quando l'amicizia si dissipa in più dimensioni e comincia a rappresentare dentro di sé tutte le forme delle relazioni sociali; accade ad esempio che l'amicizia scopra l'utile concreto degli amici; quando si è amici in funzione dell'utilità (e non il contrario) accade che la dissimmetria intervenga a deludere quella quota, spesso crescente, di utile che ci si aspetta dall'amico. La delusione travolge l'amicizia e la trasforma nel luogo del conflitto e della *re-criminazione*.

The same author points out that the text guides us through the opaque side of everyday life in which feelings are exposed to the possibility of risks. In this interregnum, friendship and trust distance themselves and ethics slowly and silently gives way to law. This is emphasised in the observation that friendship and law have a complex relationship in the Aristotelian discourse[10]: "One might think that, just as justice is of two kinds, unwritten (*àgraphon*) and written in law (*katà nòmon*), so too is friendship that tends towards utility of two kinds, moral (etikè) and legal (*nomikè*)" (Resta 2009, p. 54).

In moral friendship, we do not have an "explicit pact", trust exists and is implied. Trust here serves as a "moral mediation", with no other means necessary

---

[10] This is also the opinion of Ota Leonardis when he emphasises: "il diritto intrattiene rapporti complicati com la fiducia" (Leonardis 2009, p. 121).

to ensure smooth communication between friends. The risk of disappointment from unmet expectations in the relationship is zero, and therefore, as Aristotle once said, referring to moral friendship: "if men are friends, there is no need for justice" (Aristotle 2005, n.p.).

The success of the Aristotelian discourse shows us that there is an inclusive relationship between friendship and justice, in the sense that the latter becomes superfluous when the former is true and disinterested. Unfortunately, this is not enough: the ethics of friendship is that of intentions, of the ethical stance adopted by a friend who gives and receives. Trust is placed in the intention and it differentiates true friendship from that which is said to be self-interested. When trust fades, when expectations are not met, the law steps in and trust becomes influential for matters pertaining to it, but only a detail concerning the friendship relationship. Thus,

> sembrerebbe in tal caso che si affidi al diritto perchè si è persa la fiducia in altre istanze di controllo della correttezza dei comportamenti e del rispetto degli accordi – istanze morali, di deontologia professionale, di reputazione ecc. – e faccia presa un senso diffuso di irresponsabilità, tale per cui chiunque, individuo e sopratutto organizzazione, appena può ne approfita ... (Leonardis 2009, p. 122)

It is in this sense that in legal friendship we relegate to the Law the guarantee of fulfilling the established obligations, which in moral friendship is not necessary, as non-compliance is out of the question due to the ethical and morally accepted implication by friends. It is at this moment that friendship becomes juridified and we work with the notion of trust. When the expectation of trust in the fulfilment of the other's obligations is not realised, the law intervenes to make the disappointment bearable and to resolve the conflicts arising from it. Thus, trusting in the other's word is to exclude oneself from the legal system (Riccobono 2009).

Niklas Luhmann (2002, p. 54) asserted that the law is established in a society that has already tasted moral trust. Therefore, just like friendship is a political concept integral to the community, so is trust. These are two important elements that make community existence possible. The crisis involving this statement occurs precisely because both no longer have ethics and morals as their basis, but the law, the codified right. Thus, friendship is currently translated as solidarity and trust. Both are especially guaranteed in the contractual sphere by good faith.[11] Therefore, it is possible to affirm that "juridified trust will need binary codes: it will become *bona* because, and while, it will have to relate to *mala fides*" (Resta 2009, p. 60).

What is noticeable is that neither friendship and, consequently, trust remain as conceived in ancient Greek and Roman societies, but as legal principles whose security and guarantee of respectability are no longer based on ethical/moral relations but on the state guarantee of the judiciary.

Trust is in crisis. This crisis has two fundamental aspects: firstly, we observe a crisis of horizontal trust in the relationships between citizens, identifying the

[11] Good faith means "mutual loyalty, clarity, correctness" skills necessary to implement a congruent linguistic communication before being legal as well as satisfying "a spirit of cooperation for the fulfilment of mutual expectations" (Betti 1971, pp. 390–391).

dismantling of community ties, including, for example, ties of friendship and solidarity; subsequently, there is a crisis of vertical trust, that is, a clear and growing distrust between the citizen and the institutions to which he connects, including jurisdiction. The first aspect, pertaining to horizontal relationships and moral/ethical trust, can only be recovered through the implementation of a new paradigm in relationships between individuals. In the second aspect, regarding vertical relationships, there is a search for the application of the law and rights to guarantee their principles.

The main consequence of the loss of trust as an ethical/moral relationship is recourse to the law and the judiciary. Thus, the abuse of rights and the juridification of the social strongly contribute to the entropy of trust. A community that predominantly uses the law to resolve its conflicts is less trustworthy and less capable of producing trust.

The ancient connotation of friendship and trust has been lost, but the relationship Their policy, born and maintained, was still guaranteed by codes and laws. Nowadays, there are movements that seek to reclaim this ethical connotation of friendship and all its derivatives: trust, solidarity, fraternity, otherness. This is the debate that unfolds below.

References

Books

Arendt H (2004) Condição humana. 10th edn. Forense, Rio de Janeiro

Aristóteles (1996) Os pensadores. Nova Cultural, São Paulo

Aristóteles (2005) L'amicizia. Lorenzo Barbera Editore S.r.l, Siena

Bauman Z (2001) Modernidade líquida. Tradução de Plínio Dentzien. Jorge Zahar, Rio de Janeiro

Betti E (1971) Interpretazione della legge e degli atti giuridici (teoria generale e dogmática). 2. ed. Milano: Giuffrè

Cicero MT (1993) L'amcizia. Newton Compton editori s.r.l, Roma

Cícero MT (2001) Da amizade. Martins Fontes, São Paulo

Cicero MT (2004) I doveri. Saggio introdutivo e note di Emanuele Narducci. 1st edn. Libri e Grandi Opere, Milano

Elias N (1994) O processo civilizador: uma história dos costumes, vol 2. Jorge Zahar, Rio de Janeiro

Elias N (2001) A sociedade de corte. Jorge Zahar, Rio de Janeiro

Foucault M (2004) Ética, sexualidade e política. Forense universitária, Rio de Janeiro

Foucault M (2005) História da sexualidade, 16th edn. Graal, Rio de Janeiro

La Boétie E de (1999) O Discurso da servidão voluntária. Brasiliense, São Paulo

Leonardis O (2009) Appunti su fiducia e diritto. Tra giuridificazione e dirito informale. In: Parolechiave: nuova serie di problemi del socialismo. Roma: Carocci Editore, v. 42, dicembre

Luhmann N (2002) La fiducia. Bologna: Il Mulino

Ortega F (2002) Genealogias da Amizade. Coleção Políticas de Imanência. Iluminuras, São Paulo

Platão (1995) Lísis. UnB, Brasília

Resta E (2009) Le regole della fiducia. Laterza, Roma

Resta E (2020) O Direito Fraterno. Essere nel Mondo, Santa Cruz do Sul
Riccobono F (2009) Fidúcia, fede, diritto. In: Parolechiave: nuova serie di problemi del socialismo. Roma: Carocci Editore, v. 42, dicembre
Schaefer S (2010) A concepção de amizade na Ética a Nicômaco de Aristóteles. In: Albornoz S, Gai PE Ó Meus Amigos, Não Há Amigos! Reflexão sobre amizade, Editora Movimento/Edunisc, Santa Cruz do Sul
Vernant JP (1989) L'individu, la mort, l'amour. Soi-même et l'autre em Grèce ancienne. Gallimard, Paris

Chapter 3
The Political Game of Friend/Enemy Mediated by Fraternal Communication

Currently, it is possible to question the importance and even the necessity of discussing fraternity. Moreover, the ability to relate fraternity to the theory and practice of politics has also been lost. Indeed, studying the relationship between fraternity and politics has never been considered an attractive topic. Freedom and equality often appear in this debate, but fraternity is always forgotten.

The French Revolution and its participants, who produced the triad "freedom, equality, and fraternity"—universal principles of a political nature—, gradually purged fraternity from its context, focusing only on the first two. In this sense, fraternity began to be seen as the poor cousin, "the cousin from the countryside" (Resta 2020, p. 11), gradually assuming other connotations[1]: religious, consanguineous, or in the form of "sectarian ties, within secret organisations, or those that place levels of secrecy alongside others of a public nature—such as freemasonry—and seek to strengthen their own network of economic and political power" (Baggio 2008, p. 20).

In addressing the theme of friendship as a social cement enabling appropriate conflict management, (Resta 2004, p. 09) refers to fraternal law, noting that "fraternity has a vaguely anachronistic sense", as it takes us back to the Enlightenment revolution scenario. However, it is not with this connotation that fraternal law is intended to be addressed, (nor was it how Eligio Resta conducted his text) since when said in that way, fraternity "hinted at many things, but remained in a state of silent nod". Thus, "it confirmed above all the game of belonging of individuals, of flesh and blood men and women, to the territory of birth . . . ". Consequently, "it linked by separating, included by excluding: the feeling of fraternity towards other nations, from the people of one nation, to the people of other nations." (Resta 2004, p. 09) Thus, it opened the cosmopolitan scene only to immediately close it within the confines of national belonging. Therefore, the anachronism of fraternity can be translated as a

[1] This statement is merely illustrative as the present study does not aim to deeply investigate fraternity in the Christian/family/associative context.

© The Author(s), under exclusive license to Springer Nature Switzerland AG 2025
F. M. Spengler, *Community Conflict Mediation*,
https://doi.org/10.1007/978-3-032-09873-3_3

contretemps, in the exact sense of "going against time", in the sense of rowing against the current or perhaps interrupting the linearity that goes from beginning to end.

Following the words of Resta (2020), the aim here is to discuss fraternity and, consequently, fraternal law as a result of friendship and as that which abandons the closed borders of citizenship, respecting human rights and which, by returning to the binomial constituted by law and fraternity, puts back into play a model of the rule of the political community: a model not victorious, but possible.[2] In this way, the author proposes a return to a "conventional model of law, 'sworn together' among brothers and not imposed, as it is said, by the 'warlord father'. Sworn together, but not produced in 'collusion' (Resta 2020, p. 15). Therefore, it is decisively non-violent—that is, capable of not appropriating that violence which it claims to combat" (Resta 2020, p. 15).

In this sense, the present text aims to delimit, at first, fraternity as a fundamental category integrated and integrated by the concept of friendship. Subsequently, the links between the concept of fraternity, otherness and solidarity will be investigated from a perspective that prioritises the multifaceted relationships existing between these categories and community conflict mediation.

Furthermore, the debate will move towards investigating the possibilities and prerogatives of fraternity as a political category, considering that in this field it needs to fulfil at least two important conditions: *a)* at first, fraternity becomes a constitutive part of the criterion for political decision-making, contributing to determining, along with freedom and equality, the method and contents of politics itself; *b)* subsequently, it can influence how the other two political categories, freedom and equality, are interpreted. Indeed, a dynamic interaction between the three principles must be ensured, without neglecting any of them, in all public spheres: economic policy, the legislature and the judiciary, and international law (Baggio 2008, p. 23).

The chapter is divided into three parts and debates, in the first of them, fraternity and the political game of social exclusion/inclusion, especially pointing to the limits and connections between expressions such as: enemy and criminal. The following subsection discusses fraternity as a legal category/demand and the importance of this debate in contemporary times. Finally, it addresses conflict mediation as a strategy to implement/recompose social communication.

This, then, is the chapter presented.

3.1 Friendship as Politics and Its Relations with Fraternity

Many thinkers,[3] among them Derrida (2003), debate friendship and community as the central point of their works. This is an attempt to reclaim the political "within" and for "the" community, rethinking and rebuilding it alongside

---

[2] On this subject, it is important to read DERRIDA, Jacques. Politics of Friendship. 2003.

[3] It is possible to mention here Maurice Blanchot, Michel Foucault, Gilles Deleuze; Felix Guattari. However, at this moment the debate will be centred on the work of Jacques Derrida.

democracy. In this way, friendship would be shifted from the private sphere, from intimacy—a place to which it was banished—especially by Christianity, which broadened friendship and emptied it of the political—to the world, the public, the community.

One could generally explain, for example, the history of fraternity in social systems as a history marked and traversed at all times by continuous paradoxical movements, of increasing differentiations of the community and of increasing tendencies towards unitary recompositions. This explains why the "being-in-common" of brothers who share birth, is represented as the place of peace and war, of concord and conflict, then, as the place of ambivalence par excellence. It thus represents both the space of solidarity and that of enmity and rivalry, that of Antigone and Cain: the biblical expression "brothers in arms" can be understood both in the sense that one is an enemy despite being a brother, and that one is an enemy precisely because they are brothers (Resta 2020, p. 26).

In these terms, the work *Politiques de L'amitie* (Derrida 2003) presents itself as a text of an evidently political nature, as it proposes a debate on the (im)possibility of a new experience of friendship, which in itself represents a challenge to traditional ways of thinking about the political. Thus, the friendship that can be reviewed and perhaps rebuilt from Derrida's text would constitute an exercise of the political as a form and means of retracing and reinventing it.

Derrida's philosophy highlights in Kant's Enlightenment thought the respect as a condition for true friendship. Kant (1986) gives originality to this concept, linking it to another important word in the context of friendship: responsibility. In this way, it is understood that there is no respect without a clear vision, for which a certain distance and personal space is necessary; similarly, there can be no responsibility without response, without communication, without this receiving that takes time, that makes one lose it to later gain it.

Therefore, in Kant (1986) we read about the impossibility of friendship without respect for the other, which can be translated as a "morally good will", a virtue, translated by a *próté philía,* a virtuous friendship, between good and virtuous men.

Thus, from Kant (1986) to Derrida (2003), based on Aristotle (Aristóteles 1996), respecting a friend is not necessarily respecting the law; friendship exists only as far as the person and not as far as the law. The latter can only be the cause of moral respect (Derrida 2003).

In Aristotelian texts, Derrida (2003) finds, and based on them works, the connection between the just, friendship and community division. In this context, Derrida outlines two consequences of friendship: (a) it is a relationship irreducible to the instrument (technical dimension); (b) on the other hand, it is destined for democracy.[4] Not that this is firm as a law, but it would be a tendency, a proportional relationship; because there are more common things where citizens

[4] At this point, Derrida links fraternity and democracy, stating that the latter has rarely been determined without the brotherhood or fraternity.

are equal, and community sharing implies more law, more contract, more convention, therefore, democracy is more favourable to friendship than tyranny. The paternal relationship is monarchical, and the relationship between man and his wife is aristocratic, but the political, which is often translated as democratic, is the relationship between brothers, the equality of fraternity. *A politeia* is a matter of brothers (Albornoz 2010, pp. 144–145).

Thus, gradually the friend appears in the discourses of friendship in the figure of the brother. From Aristotle (Aristóteles 1996), democratic friendship constitutes a relationship of fraternisation: friendship is, in principle, democratic because it is fraternal. Despite the great discourses of friendship having linked the brother-friend to democracy, to justice, to virtue and to political reason, this identification of the brother with the friend or the enemy is not evident (Ortega 2000, p. 60).

However, the universalist ideal of fraternity excludes, in principle, any enmity or hostility, which is undoubtedly a utopia. We must not forget that the most violent, bitter and intense hostilities occur more frequently among individuals who present ethnic, ideological similarities or who are related than among strangers. Precisely for this reason, the supposed universalism of the fraternal discourse encloses a particularist logic that historically enabled the emergence of nationalist, xenophobic and populist policies (Ortega 2000, pp. 63–64).

Derrida (2003) considers that it is perhaps impossible to identify the concept of fraternity with the *philia* of the Greeks, if we still know what *philia* was for the Greeks, but it is still problematic to approximate it to *freundschaft, friendship,* or even *amitié,* in modern languages. In the same vein, Eligio Resta emphasises that "the symbolic construction of an identity perceived through threat (not alien, moreover, to the entire history of Europe) records a progressive approximation between fraternity and the Greek concept of friendship (*philía*)" (Resta 2007, p. 591).

It is in this sense that Derrida's proposal seeks to unmask all philosophical discourses of friendship as discourses of fraternity as a delimiting movement, proposing to think of friendship beyond it. What Derrida (2003) intends is to point out the connection between friendship, fraternity and democracy. His proposal is to present a new politics of friendship (im-possible?). To achieve this, he seeks to deconstruct the link between friendship and fraternity, present in all discourses, to create the space for a new friendship and a new democracy beyond fraternity, beyond fraternisation. A "democracy to come", that does justice to this friendship, as *perhaps*. A democracy without autochthony and eugenics, free from its familiar and androcentric figures, without ceasing to be a democracy. Is it possible? *Perhaps* (Ortega 2000, p. 60).

The deconstruction of friendship and the search for a new politics of friendship that goes beyond fraternity, that is, beyond the common understanding of democracy reveals the dangerous "perhaps" of an (im)possibility. It is at this point that

Derrida uses Schmitt (1992) to emphasise that opposition, that is, enmity, makes and delimits the political. It is not from friendship that it is born, but from the existence of the enemy. Therefore, if we wanted to derive a politics of friendship more than war, we would still have to understand what "friend" means. Now, the meaning of "friend" is determined only in the oppositional distinction "friend-enemy" (Derrida 2003, p. 252).

Thus, there must be real struggle for the ultimate logic of the political configuration that opposes friend/enemy to manifest. It is from the perspective of this extreme possibility that men's lives are enriched with their specifically political tension. A world where the possibility of struggle had been entirely removed and banned, a definitively pacified planet, would be a world without discrimination against friend/enemy and consequently a world without politics. The political phenomenon could not be grasped by abstracting this real possibility of grouping into friends and enemies, whatever the consequences for the evaluation of the political from a religious, moral, aesthetic or economic point of view (Wermuth and Spengler 2019).

Derrida's discourse reinforces the dizzying process of hyperbolisation to which friendship and fraternity are exposed. There is always something more fraternal than the brother, more friendly than the friend, more just than justice or law—and the measure is given precisely by the immensity, by the immeasurability of this "more". The mechanism of hyperbolisation (because there is mechanics and technique in this regularity) works all this semantics between the strict sense and the proper sense. Thus, true fraternity, fraternity in the proper sense would be universal, spiritual, symbolic, infinite, the fraternity of oath, etc. and not the fraternity in the strict sense, that of the "natural" brother (as if this ever existed), of the virile brother, in opposition to the sister, of the determined brother, in this family, in this nation, in this language. And what we highlight here from fraternity, as the dominant scheme of friendship, carries in this, as in all values associated with its disconcerting hyperbole (Derrida 2003, p. 244).

For Derrida (2003), the philosophical discourses of friendship reproduced the logic of the epitaph. This means the possibility of a friendship beyond death. The history of the continuous quotation attributed to Aristotle by Montaigne (2012): "Oh, my friends, there are no friends". Thus, to love the friend implies the commitment to love him beyond life or death. In this way, according to Derrida's logic, digging into the discourses of friendship the logic of the epitaph allows to point out two issues: (a) reference to symmetry and equality in the relationship of friendship; (b) to the theme of mourning and its political implications. Consequently, friendship becomes the political mourning for the friend-*brother*.

This relationship between the friend-brother and between the friend/enemy founds and represents, as pointed out earlier, the political. The way this relationship takes place within fraternity and in the elaboration of a fraternal law is the subject of the next item.

3.2 Fraternity in the Face of Social Exclusion and the Political Game of the Friend/Enemy Brother[5]

Fraternal law is that which, when equality breaks into the heart of sovereignty, seems to finally realise a symbolic project born with modernity, that of the overthrow of a paternal law, always existing, given by God, tradition, nature, that is, those legacies that obstructed the imperative of transformation (Resta 1996).

In this sense, if fraternal law is the one that is born from a feeling of guilt for the beheading of the king, one cannot lose sight of Freud's work (1997) which discusses in *Totem and Taboo*. The sibling relationship suggests that siblings are those who share the same impotence and rivalry, and who vie for the father's power (or at least a portion of it).[6] In this way, they create solidarity by recognising the paternal figure and mutually desiring his death. Therefore, "from the moment the paternal function is recognised, the children are oppressed" (Enriquez 1993, p. 35). This is the father's right, who, in imposing his authority, is rejected by his children, creating the idea of collusion for the jointly committed crime.

Along the same lines, Enriquez (1993, p. 36) discusses the primordial time—governed by the infinite repetition of the same acts and thoughts, of the horde, led by an omnipotent tyrant, characterised by the refusal of love and the handling of force—, to the time of history made possible by this first infraction of order, which was the *unanimous decision of the crime*. As the author states, "we move from a *world* of power relations to a world of alliance and solidarity relations (even if these remain fragile), from a *state* of nature to a state of law, where the law is embodied by the one who represented total arbitrariness in life". In this context, this "creation of the social is accompanied (preceded—followed) by the expression of complex feelings: love, veneration, friendship, guilt. The birth of the group is inconceivable without the corresponding emergence of feelings".

Consequently, of all these feelings born from the formation of the Rule of Law, one of them deserves special attention, because, if fraternal law is conventional and non-violent, it is important to consider it permeated by the law of friendship which finds "in modern codification processes the formula of the imperative of fraternity in the face of a political game, built on the known opposition of the *friend-enemy*".[7]

---

[5] This ambivalence in the figure of the brother who can also be an enemy comes from the texts of Eligio Resta in which he states: "l'espressione biblica: "fratelli nemici" può essere intesa tanto nel senso che si è nemici nonostante si sai fratelli, quando che si è nemici própio perché fratelli." (Resta 2007, p. 588.)

[6] Questo spiega, tra l'altro, perchè l' "essere-in-comune" dei fratelli che condividono la nascita, venga rappresentato nello stesso tempo come il luogo della pace e della guerra, della concordia e del conflitto, dunque, come luogo dell'ambivalenza per eccellenza. (Resta 2007, p. 588.)

[7] "The concepts of friend and enemy must be understood in their concrete, existential sense, and never as metaphors or symbols; they should not be diluted by mixing them with economic, moral or other representations, nor especially interpreted psychologically in a private-individualistic sense, as if they expressed private feelings and tendencies. These concepts are neither normative oppositions nor spiritual oppositions". (Free translation from: Derrida 2003, p. 250).

However, friendship does not follow a linear path between collective virtue and quality, which "wanes in the relationship and oscillates from the public life plane to the most intimate private sphere". The more friendship loses "its character of spontaneous mortar of society", the more it needs to be prescribed by a law that contains ethical-religious imperatives, but mainly legal ones. Thus, friends are no longer necessarily those linked by fraternal ties and solidarity, as they evade the bond and daily reciprocity, sharing life without sharing it (Resta 2004, pp. 20–21).

The genesis of friendship is divided into contingent and transcendent, as it depends on chance and the event where it develops. Therefore, the support community has already lost its universalist sense and has confined itself to numerically measurable relations of a defined friendship, consequently, "we are friends because there are enemies, we are friends because we choose each other to oppose other forms of imposed or involuntary relations" (Resta 2004, p. 31). These relations determine a character of inclusion/exclusion to friendship, including the friend and excluding the enemy, and becoming a normal improbability.

The relations between friends and enemies in the same territory come—according to Freud in his text *Considerations on War and Death* (1915)—, established within each nation, by its moral rules, which individuals should adjust to. These rules brought great delimitations and a marked renunciation of man's natural instincts. Such norms are considered the basis of the civilised state, being defended by it. Therefore, whoever complied with the norms was the friend and whoever did not respect them was the criminal, or rather, whoever submitted to them was the friend and whoever repudiated them was considered the criminal.

Discussing the relationship of belonging and enmity, Freud (1997) points out that there are three essential taboos: the enemies foreign to the tribe, the leaders foreign to the group, and the dead foreign to life. Having a character outside the norms considered normal, the power that these foreigners can exert over individuals is delimited by the fact that the enemy kills us, the leader subjugates us, and the dead haunt us and call us.

The relations of friendship/enmity between the citizen and the foreigner have a close link with the institution of hospitality (*xenia*) which can be summarised as a way of relating to foreigners, including a series of reciprocal obligations and benefits. This is because the laws of hospitality impose restrictions on hospitality itself; thus, it is always "the law and the laws that constitute, impose, determine, condition and delimit relations with the foreigner" (Ortega 2002, p. 18). According to Derrida (1997, pp. 69 and 131–132) this "becoming law of justice", is characteristic of the laws of hospitality, having "the same *predominance* in the structure of the right to hospitality and the relationship with the foreigner, whether guest or enemy". It is a "conjugal, paternal and phallogocentric model. It is the family despot, the father, the husband, the master, the owner of the house, who makes the laws of hospitality" (Ortega 2002, p. 18).

Thus, the French author points to the fact that an unconditional hospitality law could require breaking with hospitality laws established through a pact, an alliance, or a contract. A fair hospitality that encourages breaking with hospitality as a law or right, presupposes observing the social and family status of the contractors, as well as the possibility of calling them "by their name, of having a name, of being subjects of law, addressed and liable, accountable, responsible, endowed with a nameable identity, with a proper name" (Derrida 1997, p. 27).

Therefore, establishing a hospitality pact by imposing conditions on it is a way of assimilating the other, suppressing their uniqueness, their otherness, however, "assimilating the other" is not enough, it is necessary for them to be welcomed and become part of our space, to think/act differently is to assimilate the other and integrate them. Acting differently and not being hospitable.

However, the difficulty of integrating the other and the attitude aimed at assimilating them is an attitude that ignores their otherness and is often assumed because the foreigner can destroy my space, question my identity, and even impose their culture or language. So, a doubt persists: "how to create a hospitality relationship that is not imposed as assimilation or acculturation, but that is also not simply the occupation of my space by the other?" (Ortega 2002, p. 20). Perhaps the best hypothesis to answer this question is constant negotiation, without the rigidity of inflexible and predetermined rules, in the form of an empty programme, according to Derrida (1997, p. 33) precisely for this reason the negotiation must take place at every moment, constantly. Thus, the most appropriate rules must be invented every second regardless of the risks involved which becomes very dangerous.

When it comes to hospitality/otherness, the name is a fundamental issue. This is because demanding someone's name presupposes attributing an identity and a responsibility to the foreigner, who will answer before the law and before the guests, as a witness in a court; it is precisely the name that constitutes them as a subject of law. The other, the one who does not have a name is excluded from the embrace of *xenia*. Consequently, the friend/enemy discriminations run throughout classical Greece through a binary code: friendship inside, enmity outside.

However, nowadays friendship has ceased to be the cement of society because it is covered by enmity, it cannot be lost sight of that

> The political community is, in fact, described as the place where the enemy, by convention, is no longer internal, but external. The internal enemy, through a complex metamorphosis of semantics, has been assigned the role of "criminal" or political opponent, or even, minority: the transitions are, obviously, all rich and refined, and are not even sudden. They presuppose that a "natural contract" (as defined by Michel Serres) is already underway, by which one "belongs" to a nation, and therefore all its laws are accepted (Resta 2004, p. 34).

What indicates the relationship of belonging between an individual and a certain fraternity, is their birth code, which links to an obedience in exchange for citizenship, so that when linked, one can be, in case of transgression, at most a criminal, but never an enemy.[8] This happens because precisely by knowing the law in all its validity the

[8] The internal enemy is metabolised and neutralised through its transformation into a criminal, the external enemy remains potentially such. Fraternity closes in the more or less small homelands of nation-states and international law continues to be the place of variable and fleeting fraternity towards states that, when not enemies, are neutral, allies or recipients of paternalistic interference. (Resta 2007, p. 590.)

enemy steals and then flees. They know that they have committed an act contrary to the social rules of their group and that is why they hide (Resta 2020, p. 91).

This link between men through obedience to the rules and, consequently, citizenship is discussed by Bauman (2004, p. 148) when he points to the industrial production, in the modern era, of "human waste", of social criminals, especially in two branches: a) in the function of production and reproduction of social order. In this way, the order model is selective and requires that "cut, trim, segregate, separate or extirpate parts of the human raw material that are unsuitable for the new order incapable or despised for the filling of any of its niches". These parts thus despised emerge as "waste", without utility. b) in a second moment, economic progress is envisaged, which requires "incapacitation, dismantling and final annihilation of a certain number of forms and means of human beings earning a living—modes of subsistence—that could not and would not adjust to constantly rising productivity and profitability standards." These individuals were denied access to modes of subsistence as new arrangements became necessary, becoming the "waste of economic progress".

In parallel, the human waste industry needed to find ways to deal with its waste, thus, the surpluses of humanity were deposited in large sanitary landfills, giving rise to a new character: the "human being thrown beyond the limits of human and divine laws", transforming them into a being to whom "laws do not apply and whose destruction does not entail punishments, stripped as it is of any ethical religious meaning". At this moment, the human rights of these displaced beings, treated as criminals, proved to be inhospitable land since they could not reach people who were not citizens of any modern state (Bauman 2004, p. 148).

Thus, assuming the fact that the modern state is a state that makes birth[9] The foundation of its sovereignty, for an outsider to knock on the door of the State asking for admission, they must first be subjected to the ritual of stripping, since "the nakedness of the newborn child not yet wrapped in legal-legal orders, provides the *locus* in which the sovereignty of the State's power is perpetually built, rebuilt and assisted with the help of inclusion/exclusion practices destined to all other citizenship claimants who fall under the reach of this sovereignty". Therefore, in order to belong to a certain State, and thus be included, one must first be excluded, violently, go through the "place of none", be isolated, get naked, to only then dress in the clothes of equals and be included in the group by the bonding code (Bauman 2004, pp. 150–154).

[9] Hannah Arendt addresses the three activities and their respective conditions that are intimately related to the most general conditions of human existence: "birth and death, natality and mortality. Labour ensures not only the survival of the individual, but the life of the species. Work and its product, the human artefact, lend a certain permanence and durability to the futility of mortal life and the ephemeral nature of human time. Action, insofar as it strives to found and preserve political bodies, creates the condition for remembrance, that is, for history ... Nevertheless, of the three activities, action is most intimately related to the human condition of natality; the new beginning inherent in each birth can only make itself felt in the world because the newcomer has the capacity to start something new, that is, to act." (Free translation from: Arendt 2004, pp. 16–17).

In this sense, the modern bonding code is that of the French Revolution which determines the equality of all citizens before the law, promoting the birth of constitutions that gave legal formulations to fraternity. That being said, "the fraternity of conventionally voted constitutions reopens the game of political friendship, but, obviously, does not eliminate its paradoxes." Among these paradoxes, we have that fraternal law, constituted among "equals must presuppose an original act of suppression of the father, so that there are no more tyrants, and that, therefore, carries with it this theology of violence", in a second moment, "it concerns the raison d'être of the general will, which ends, even in relation to those who were its victims, generalising the force that wins or the majority that supports it" (Resta 2004, pp. 36–36).

However, Enriquez (1993, p. 312) views with scepticism what he calls *mutual love* (in fraternity), not agreeing with the possibility of a power shared by the adherence of objectives outlined to ensure a group the non-manifestation of power of an individual or subgroup. He supports his claim by saying that if effectively the social bond is a tragic bond, and questions: how would the issue of the group's internal violence be resolved (in fraternal law)? On the other hand, he points out that the collective will needs to be expressed by the majority or by its representatives and needs to foresee the unconditional acceptance of differences, a strong capacity for communication, and finally, a certain community of culture. However, these conditions are also inherent to fraternity and can be envisaged and fostered in places where conflict resolution is operated through the use of community justice (Spengler 2018).

Consequently, for Enriquez (1993, p. 317) if the group does not achieve a sufficient degree of implication to achieve the previously set goals, the members will tend to, disconnect. But, at the same time, he questions: "are we then obliged to condemn, definitely the attempts at transformation and social renewal?" And he answers: "not at all, quite the contrary. We just wanted to highlight the stones and obstacles inherent to all work of this order and dispel the illusion . . . of the creation of a transparent society where conflicts would always find a solution . . . " That's why, even maintaining some reservations about fraternity, Enriquez recognises its importance as a way to better understand social functioning stating that we should not expect an answer to the question but a new question.

This question also arises in the context of the political theory of law in the sense of questioning the inclusion of fraternity as a category belonging to these spheres. This is the topic discussed ahead.

3.3 Fraternity as a Legal Category/Demand

As previously discussed, fraternity belongs to the triad "freedom, equality, fraternity" originating from the French Revolution. However, as a political category, it was forgotten. Losing strength, it was gradually pushed into the realm of private and religious relations.

However, in recent years, fraternity has been reclaiming its space and demonstrating its importance to the point of emerging as a requirement of politics itself. This is, above all, due to the realisation that the implementation of the other two principles that we take as a reference (freedom and equality), was incomplete or even failed. As an example, it is possible to identify two typologies of failure or limitation in the implementation of these principles (Baggio 2008, pp. 11–13):

(a) firstly, the "external" typology, that concerning the relations between the geopolitical and economic regions in which the Planet is divided and the indicators of non-development do not apply only to underdeveloped countries, but also to the most heavily industrialised, thanks to the interpenetration of the various "worlds": First, Second, Third and Fourth. However, today, there is a Third World and a Fourth within the First and Second, not composed of recent and poor immigrants, but produced by the very uncertainty of the system, that is, by the fragility that continues to accompany the implementation of the principles of freedom and equality;
(b) however, it is precisely in the "internal" typology of the most industrialised societies, in which the production of goods (material and cultural) is exorbitant in relation to the needs of the population—in front of which we would be led to think that freedom and equality were satisfactorily achieved—, that the problem presents itself in the most unexpected way; these societies continue to be permeated by wide bands of poverty, named in different ways by various scholars. Thus, society knows how to produce new "triads" from the unprecedented combinations arising from social transformations.

In the meantime, the conception of friend/enemy/criminal/foreigner pointed out above becomes clear, as within a single state,—in a geopolitical conception—there can exist, in addition to the friend and the criminal, also the enemy, who primarily inhabits another state—resides outside the borders—but who is here represented by the foreigner and the excluded. These latter, who, often without committing acts contrary to the rules (therefore they are not criminals) remain on the margins of the social system, are not recognised and not considered by it. This is an "internal" enemy/foreigner.

Thus, in addition to social inclusion (and this presupposes autonomy of choice, among other prerogatives), fraternity, as a category and political demand, aims to enable happiness, which, even though understood as the result of personal pursuit, is linked to a quest that also pertains to the public space.

Modern society proclaims the right to happiness: this right is not only about improving the standard of living, but the degree of happiness of the men and women involved should justify (or condemn, if that degree refuses to reach ever higher levels) society and all its works. Therefore, the pursuit of happiness and the hope of success have become "the main motivation for the individual's participation in society" (Bauman 2003, p. 76).

Therefore, it is not possible to be individually happy within a socially unhappy community. The society/community in which the individual is inserted also offers its share of contribution (or not!) in the construction of their happiness and well-being. The formula that currently emerges regarding the (changeable) scope of the pursuit of happiness can be translated by the terms "security" (in place of freedom), "parity" (in place of equality) and "network" (in place of fraternity) (Baggio 2008, p. 14).

Here the word "network" is understood as the possibility offered by technology for any individual to establish a set of virtual relationships, which remain at the disposal of the subject who builds them. Consequently, in this network "there is no relationship with a reality that resists and opposes, there is no true relationship with the other—there is no real otherness—, because, when the individual gets bored, they disconnect". Consequently, the network, understood in this sense, "is an expansion of the self, which replaces real human relationships" (Baggio 2008, pp. 14–15).

This interpretation of fraternity which—from the point of view of Morin (2005)—highlights the need not to renounce the construction of a truly human society, gives body to the idea that we are experiencing a kind of deficit in political reflection, a deficit that is also manifested in practice, and that can only be filled by the broad recovery of the principle of fraternity, in political and legal practice.

However, the question concerns the clear delimitation of the relations between fraternity and law. What is the link that binds fraternity and the legal world, when the first impression is that they are realities that operate in different and segmented fields? This section between law and fraternity is a widely held belief: many believe that fraternity can only be spontaneous, while co-activity and coercion would be typical of law. In this case, it ends up being asserted that law is all the more necessary the less fraternity acts. And, vice versa, that a society imbued with fraternity could dispense with law (Goria 2008).

Such a conception is due to the simplistic perception that the nature of law is always conflictual and that fraternity consists in spontaneity, in harmony. Despite there being a realistic bias in this propagated understanding, this fact does not justify that fraternity and law walk in opposite directions (Spengler and Dornelles 2023).

Consequently, the answer to the coexistence of law and fraternity will depend on how law is conceived, as Goria (2008, p. 26) refers: "followers of institutional theories (. . .), who think of law as inherent to any organised social group, would have no difficulty in admitting its existence also in a completely fraternal society". According to this conception, fraternity could present itself as an experience lived with positive and enriching relationships, translated into law precisely to assume a stable and institutional character. Following this line of reasoning, perhaps the most efficient way to establish relations between fraternity and law, is not the confrontation of theories, but the reminder that fraternity has already been recognised by legal systems throughout history, among them and especially the French Revolution and also in the Universal Declaration of Human Rights. Such a provision demonstrates the political importance given to this principle integral to the triad born on the occasion of the French Revolution. This importance is currently forgotten.

However, it is not about pitting fraternity against freedom and equality, or investigating which has greater importance, but rather to dialectically articulate the three principles. In this conception, fraternity could play a political role if it is capable of interpreting and transforming the real world in which we live, thus showing a heuristic value and practical efficacy. Removed from the social scene fraternity can be rescued as a means of enabling the recognition of the other and their otherness.

Such a need arises because

> By emphasising freedom and equality at the expense of fraternity, modernity has accentuated the individualistic and selfish aspects of Human Rights, forgetting the social, fraternal and solidary character of these same Rights, which are not simply of the individual and of groups or classes, but also of the "other", the poorest, the most disadvantaged. If freedom refers to the individual in their singularity, and equality opens a social dimension that, however, remains within the identity of a certain group or social class against others, fraternity refers to the idea of an "other" who is not me or my social group, but the "different" before whom I have duties and responsibilities, and not only rights to oppose (Tosi 2009, pp. 59–60).

This is the great social challenge that currently presents itself: to overcome the merely identitarian logic, and move towards an effective and efficient recognition of alterity, diversity and reciprocity. For this to happen, it is necessary to revisit the dialectic of identity/alterity. Each human being is born in a certain geographical and social place, and this implies the assimilation of a certain language, culture and "way of being in the world", which makes him what he is. Man, indeed, is not born a man, but becomes a man. It is impossible to renounce this original identity, which is part of our human condition, as beings not totally predetermined by nature. It is necessarily built in an intersubjective confrontation between an *I* and an *other*, and between *us* and others. However, all determination is, at the same time, logical and ethical, it cannot reach the point of ignoring, in diversity, what is common, that is, identity (Tosi 2009, p. 61).

The construction of identity takes place in the dialectical relationship between subjectivity and alterity. This relationship "can be merely negative: the other is seen as a non-I, different from me. If alterity remains at this level, the other will become an enemy, the adversary, the one who is hostile to me and whom I must distrust". This dialectic between subjectivity and alterity cannot be suppressed, since it is part of the construction of our identity; however, "such dialectic does not mean that the other must necessarily be seen as an enemy, ignoring the common human condition in which we all are" (Tosi 2009, p. 61).

The forgetting of our condition of humanity, of common beings with the same needs and the attribution to the other of the label of enemy demonstrates "the disembodied individualism of existence that always dispenses with, the presence of the other to constitute us as identity" (Warat 2004, p. 114).

This individualism places itself at the centre of the modern human game and in the words of Canetti (1995) it is portrayed in an isolated, solid, individualised body. This is so precisely because the "dimension of solidity is, strangely, related to loneliness as much as to solidarity" (Resta 2020, p. 21). All these words have a common root that refers to being alone, isolated, but also refers to the compact character and indivisibility:

> from this is born both the sense of *loneliness* and the duty, if not the feeling, of *solidarity*: it does not even disturb much the fact that, in the ancient world, this double bond was filtered in a border area between economy, legal obligation and the sense of the religious dimension, by that strange Latin verb, *solari* which indicated to console, but also to reimburse, to remunerate something from which we have been deprived [. . .] Solidarity brings worlds closer while loneliness lives off separations and distances (Resta 2020, pp. 21–22).

Truly, if we direct such discussion to the legal world we see "an autistic individualism that formed the idea of an autistic subject of law". We come across a "legal conception based on a proprietary-possessive-manipulative individualism, which has forgotten the other, which has lost something that is built with the other, by the presence of another in the experience" (Warat 2004, p. 114).

Therefore, the question that arises is: how to overcome this negative dialectic of alterity? And Giuseppe Tosi responds by proposing to promote a "dialectic of intersubjectivity, in which the other is not recognised as an enemy, that is, simply as a non-I, but as another I: 'I myself as another'".[10] It is in this sense that "recognising the other as myself means overcoming a purely negative dialectic of alterity, to achieve common recognition of belonging, which is part of our human condition" (Tosi 2009, p. 63).

Precisely for this reason, it is necessary to recognise the importance of a cosmopolitan Law that is concerned with ecological issues, issues of war and peace, that seeks universal human development, that is, that defends issues that go beyond the borders of States and necessarily overcome the merely individualistic logic, the logic of personal interest, of group, class or ethnicity. This proposal overcomes the logic of "belonging" to protect the logic of the "human", of "being with the other" and not "against the other".

In this "being with the other" social mediation practices emerge as a tool for exercising cosmopolitan citizenship, as they serve to educate, facilitate, and help produce differences and make decisions, without the intervention—somewhat undemocratic—of third parties who decide for the affected parties in the conflict. Therefore, to talk about identity and otherness is to talk, in a correlated way, about the capacity for autonomy and communication with others. This topic will be the subject of discussion later.

3.4 Mediation as a Strategy to Depolarise Social Communication Outlining Fraternity and Otherness

The fraternal community, as previously stated, is not a place of goodness by definition, it is merely a common space. Therefore, the same brothers who compose it can generate as much threat as fraternity. All this because "it is not enough to be brothers to share fraternity, just as it is not enough to be men to have humanity"

[10] This is Paul Ricoeur's formula. (Baggio 2008).

(Resta 2007, p. 589). Thus, connecting fraternity and conflict Resta (2020) states that brothers/enemies are united precisely by what separates them: the conflict. He also emphasises that the oldest form of community is precisely that community of the conflicting parties who no longer have the ability to communicate adequately.

Mediation is a way to establish community communication broken between citizens or groups due to the antagonistic position established by the conflict (Spengler 2012). Being an exchange communication in which the conflicting parties stipulate what each one is responsible for in resolving the conflict at hand, mediation facilitates the expression of dissent by defining a vehicle that can manage disagreement and reach a communicative understanding. Indeed, the main challenge that mediation faces is not to generate warm and cosy relationships, litigation-free societies or a harmonious world order. Instead, considering the endemic nature of conflict, perhaps its main challenge is to find mechanisms that enable a peacefully communicative coexistence.

Thus, if it is through dialogue that the foundations of conflict arise, then dialogue may be the best option for dealing with conflicting realities. However, despite the broad meaning attached to the term "dialogue", there is little value in invoking its power; more formally, dialogue simply means "a conversation between two or more people". It is necessary to distinguish between specific forms of dialogue, as not all dialogic processes can be useful to reduce the potential for hostility, conflict and aggression. Indeed, conversations dominated by exchanges of criticism, threats and litigious demands may only exacerbate the conflict. What is intended is transformative dialogue, that which can be translated into any form of exchange that can transform a relationship. For example, transformative dialogue can be applied whenever between individuals who are committed to separate, antagonistic and conflicting realities and who intend to transform it into a relationship in which common and solidifying realities are being built (Gergen 1999, pp. 30–31).

All this happens because to establish a transformative dialogue and restore/establish broken or hitherto non-existent communication, it is necessary to strip oneself of prejudices and inflexible posture and look at the other with a minimum of sensitivity and willingness to understand them (Spengler 2021).

We need to escape from "communication alienating life". Among these forms of communication, we find moralising judgments that imply a wrong or evil nature of people and that do not act in consonance with our values. The product of these judgments are phrases or thoughts surrounded by guilt, insult, depreciation, labelling, criticism … This form of communication traps us in a world of ideas that divide right and wrong, a world of judgment and classification. In this sense, making comparisons is also a form of alienating communication that judges the other (Rosenberg 2006, pp. 37–38).

The problem is that when we find faults in others, we begin to erect a wall between us. By blaming, I position myself as someone who knows everything and who is completely upright and the other as a flawed being who is subject to my judgment. The other is constituted as an object of contempt, subject to correction, while I remain worthy of praise and powerful. In this way, I alienate and, in the Western tradition, hostility is a normal reaction. The problem is intensified in the case of antagonistic groups, as each of them can blame the other—the poor will blame the rich for exploitation, while the rich will blame the poor for their indolence.[11]

In parallel, another way to maintain alienating communication is to deny the responsibility that each one has for their actions, feelings and thoughts. Thus, I deny my responsibility every time I attribute my actions to[12]: (a) vague and impersonal forces; (b) our condition, diagnosis, personal history or psychological; (c) actions of others; (d) orders from authorities; (e) group pressure; (f) policies, rules and institutional regulations; (g) roles determined by sex, age and social position; (h) uncontrollable impulses (Rosenberg 2006, pp. 42–43).

This responsibility for feelings, thoughts and actions should also be reflected in communication since announcing to others our desires as if they were a demand is another form of language that blocks compassionate communication. Most of us grew up using a language that encourages us to label, judge, compare, demand ... Such form of alienating communication originates from society based on hierarchy and domination. Wherever there is a large number of People who find themselves dominated by a small number are of interest to the few that the many are "educated" based on moralising judgments of "wrong", "should", "I have to" (Elias 1994, 2001). This way of thinking transfers responsibility and the possibility of choices to the minority, alienating the majority.

Emmanuel Lévinas reinforces this statement by weaving together important concepts for the present text such as "other", "face" and "responsibility". Thus: the encounter with the Other is immediately my responsibility for him. Responsibility for the neighbour is, undoubtedly, the serious name of what is called love of the neighbour, love without Eros, charity, love in which the ethical moment dominates the passionate moment, love without concupiscence. I do not like the word love very much, it is worn out and adulterated. Let's talk about an assumption of the destiny of the other. This is the "vision" of the Face, and it applies to the first one that appears. [...] justice is, therefore, prior to the assumption of the other's destiny. I must pass judgement where I should first of all assume responsibilities. [...] But it is always from the Face, from the responsibility for the Other, that justice appears, which involves judgement and comparison, comparison of what, in principle, is incomparable, for each being is unique; every Other is unique [...] (Lévinas 2005, p. 144 and 14).

---

[11] "[...] Violence is born from the disqualification of the other, the removal of the other's human characteristics, to highlight the negative aspects and, thus, dehumanise them." (Free translation from: Tosi 2009, pp. 61–62).

[12] "To be an individual *de jure* means not having anyone to blame for one's own misery, it means not seeking the causes of one's own defeats except in one's own indolence and laziness, and not seeking any other remedy except to try with more and more determination." (Free translation from: Bauman 2001, p. 48).

To "embrace" responsibility instead of "denying" it we can replace a language that implies lack of choice with one that recognises this possibility. But these choices must also respect the other. It is necessary to respect the alterity that exists in the other.

Therefore, to speak of alterity is to say much more than to refer to a cooperative, solidary procedure, of mutual mediation. We are talking about a possibility of transforming the conflict and of transforming ourselves in the conflict, all thanks to the assisted possibility of being able to look at ourselves from the other's point of view, and to put ourselves in his place to understand him and ourselves … Finally, it is alterity, otherness as a possibility of transforming the conflict, producing, in the same, the difference with the other … in this sense, we also speak of otherness or alterity: the revaluation of the other of the conflict to the detriment of the excessive privilege granted to the ways of saying of the law, in litigation (Warat 2004, p. 62).

In this sense, the lessons of Buber (2004) should be recovered. According to the Buberian vision, in the various types of I-Thou relationship, man is considered as an end and not as a means. Life is realised in the concreteness of "everyday". The author presents the word as being dialogical. Thus, the primordial category of the dialogicity of the word is the "between". More than an objective analysis of the logical or semantic structure of language, which would make the word a simple given, Buber developed a true ontology of the word attributing to it, as a speaking word, the sense of being a bearer of being. It is through it that man introduces himself into existence. It is not man who leads the word, but it is she who keeps him in being (Lévinas 2005, p. 32). For Buber the spoken word is an effective, effective and updating attitude of man's being. It is an act of man by which he makes himself man and situates himself in the world with others. The intention is to unveil the existential meaning of the word which, by the intentionality that animates it, is the ontological principle of man as a dialogical and dia-personal being. The principle words ("Grundwort") are two dynamic intentionalities that establish a direction between two poles, between two lived consciousnesses (Buber 2004, p. 30).

Therefore, in communication between two people, the dialogical is for the Buberian conception the way to explain the phenomenon of the inter-human. The expression inter-human implies the presence at the event of mutual encounter. Presence means to make present and to be made present. Reciprocity is the definitive mark of the actualisation of the phenomenon of the relationship. The "between" is thus considered as the ontological category in which the acceptance and ontological confirmation of the two poles involved in the event of the relationship is possible (Buber 2004).

It is in this line that mediation, as an ethics of alterity (Buber 2004), claims the recovery of respect and recognition of the integrity and totality of the spaces of privacy of the other, repudiating the minimum of invasive and dominating movement. The change of lenses when looking at conflicts brings a new conception of them. Disagreements are seen as alchemical opportunities, antagonistic energies as complementary and Law as solidarity. The old lenses that fragmented, classified and generated distances go to the bin. We begin to understand that each man is not an isolated monad, that they are not fragments without connection. Each one is interdependent and forced product of interactions. Society is solely the product of the complexity of these links (Warat 2004, p. 55).

Parallel to the ethics of alterity, one must think of otherness in the sense of "capturing the other": it is necessary to "capture the ethical alterity of the other and the honesty that tries to settle in his otherness". But who is the other? How to relate to him? The answers given in modernity were totalitarian, reductionist, manipulative, Eurocentric, egocentric, ethnocentric. Answers that seek to dissolve the other in his alterity, to end up devoured by the hegemonic models that belonged to the referential culture placed in a position of dominance (Warat 2004, p. 145).

Models of collective egos or standard egos. Logocentric ego, which considers alterity as a duplication of the subjectivity of each one, which, in turn, is imagined to coincide with universal reason. Our subjectivity as the measure of everything alien to us. It is the violence of reducing the other to ourselves. The new vision of otherness aims to show that it is possible to ascend from responsibility, which is even prior to our freedom, our autonomy (Warat 2004, p. 145).

Along the same line of reasoning, (Lévinas 2005, p. 31) explains the other as "the only being whose denial can only be announced as total: a homicide. The other is the only being that I can want to kill." Thus, the other is the denial that I want to annihilate, reduce, kill.

The end of mediation techniques, especially that called community mediation, is to hold the disputants accountable for the handling of the dispute that unites them from an ethics of alterity; to find, with the help of a mediator, a guarantee of success, smoothing out the edges and disagreements, understanding the repressed emotions and seeking, through communication, an understanding that meets the interests of the parties and leads to the pacification of the conflict.

In the pursuit of this understanding that leads to the pacification of the conflict, Buber proposes to man the realisation of dialogic life, an existence founded on dialogue. For the accomplishment of this task, the deep sense of the "between" here seen as the "phenomenon of response" stands out again. This response can be an act of love, not as something possessed by the I as if it were a feeling. Feelings, man possesses them; but love is something that "happens" between two human beings, beyond the I and below the You in the sphere "between" the two (Buber 2004, p. 40).

The "phenomenon of response" is essential to the relationship. Who listens if not to respond? (Buber 2004, p. 40) questions. This response holds accountable and then the "phenomenon of responsibility" is born in its two senses: first, as a response, and second, as the "obligation" to respond. For (Buber 2004, p. 40) responsibility as man's project in the history of living on a real and essential level of human life is the response to the call of the dialogic.

However, according to Lévinas's conception, (2005, p. 144) "the relationship with the other is not symmetrical", at this point the author disagrees with Martin Buber, stating that "when I say You to an I (Je) to a me (moi), would also, according to Buber, this me in front of me as the one who tells me You. There would, therefore, be a reciprocal relationship". But, Lévinas (2005, pp. 144–145) goes further saying that "instead, in the relationship to the Face, what is affirmed is the asymmetry: at the beginning, I care little about what the Other is in relation to me, this is his problem; for me, he is first of all the one for whom I am responsible".

Responsibility transcending the moral level, to a broader level, is the ethical name of reciprocity. Such reciprocity takes place in the dialogic form also by the word. Word, relationship and reciprocity are acts of man. These are the roots and foundations of the ontology of face-to-face. In this ontology, relationships occur with the "face".

It is in the Face of the Other that comes the commandment that interrupts the march of the world. Why would I feel responsible in the presence of the Face? This is Cain's answer, when he is told: "Where is your brother?" he answers: "Am I my brother's keeper?" This is the Face of the Other, taken by an image among images and when the Word of God that he carries becomes unknown. Cain's answer should not be taken as if he were mocking God, or as if he were answering like a child: "It's not me, it's the other". Cain's answer is sincere. In his answer, there is only ontology: I am me and he is him. We are ontologically separate beings (Lévinas 2005, pp. 151–152).

If the ontological relationship is based on ethics and this, as a foundation, is directed towards transformative dialogue, communication is restored, alterity and fraternity are respected, solidarity prevails.

However, there are various orientations on transformative dialogue and the restoration of communication that are relevant to the challenge of alterity. Aiming to investigate how these interactions occur and how mediation appropriates them to restore communication between the parties generating understanding, it is proposed to replace conflictive, distributive communication with cooperative and integrative communication of problems. In addition, it is possible to think about using community mediation practices to help individuals develop their capacities for self-determination/responsibility.

The opposite of mediated communication is argumentative communication. In it, the individuals participating in the discussion must make statements in which the point of view being discussed is attacked and defended … In an argumentative discussion, participants try to convince each other of the acceptability or not of the expressed opinion being discussed through argumentative statements. The specific rules of argumentation aim, therefore, at a wider (and potentially universal) application. Perhaps the clearest example of the orientation of argumentation in action is the judicial process (Gergen 1999, p. 31).

A recurring aspect in the theory of argumentation is bargaining, where each party tries to exploit the weaknesses of the other to obtain the greatest possible benefit, offering the least in return. This type of approach is widely used in disputes in the business and political fields. However, it is recommended that negotiation goes beyond the logic of the "minimum-maximum"—common in these areas—and seeks to maximise the joint satisfaction of the parties. On the other hand, bargaining should not be the foundation for resolving conflicts related to conjugality and parenthood, as these issues involve strong emotional and affective loads, making bargaining inappropriate or even unfeasible. In these situations, mediation may resort to these techniques in a limited and complement, always prioritising respect for individuals and the bond that exists between them.

The aim is to investigate how these interactions occur and how their mediation is used to re-establish communication between the parties, generating understanding. This is why the replacement of conflictive, distributive communication with cooperative and integrative communication is proposed. Furthermore, it is possible to consider the use of mediation practices to help individuals develop their capacities for self-determination/responsibility (Spengler and Neto 2022).

The conflicting parties can/should be encouraged to listen to and understand each other's thoughts and feelings about the situation, to generate multiple options, and to work together to arrive at a response that is good for both. In order to talk about the establishment/re-establishment of communication and transformative dialogue, it is necessary to start by saying no to blame and seeking relational responsibility. At this point, the difference can be the recognition that our traditions of exchange always work with the assumptions of a single truth, universal logic, winning and losing. We incessantly point out, through moralising judgements, the wrong, the different, the guilty, the true . . .

References

Books

Albornoz S (2010) Políticas da Amizade de Jacques Derrida. In: Albornoz S, Gai EP Ó Meus Amigos Não Há Amigos! Reflexão sobre amizade. Editora Movimento/Edunisc, Santa Cruz do Sul

Arendt H (2004) Condição humana, 10th edn. Forense, Rio de Janeiro

Aristóteles (1996) Os pensadores. Nova Cultural, São Paulo

Baggio AM (2008) O princípio esquecido. Cidade Nova, São Paulo

Bauman Z (2003) Comunidade: a busca por segurança no mundo atual. Jorge Zahar, Rio de Janeiro

Bauman Z (2004) Amor líquido—sobre a fragilidade dos laços humanos. Tradução de Carlos Alberto Medeiros. Jorge Zahar, Rio de Janeiro

Buber M (2004) Eu e tu, 8th edn. Centauro, São Paulo

Canetti E (1995) Massa e Poder. Companhia das Letras, São Paulo

Derrida J (1997) Del'hospitalité. Calmann-Levy, Paris

Derrida J (2003) Políticas da Amizade. Campo das Letras, Porto

Elias N (1994) O processo civilizador: uma história dos costumes, vol 2. Jorge Zahar, Rio de Janeiro

Elias N (2001) A sociedade de corte. Jorge Zahar, Rio de Janeiro

Enriquez E (1993) Da horda ao Estado: psicanálise do vínculo social. Jorge Zahar, Rio de Janeiro

Freud S (ed) (1997) O mal estar da civilização. Imago, Rio de Janeiro

Gergen KJ (1999) Rumo a um Vocabulário do Diálogo Transformador. In: Schnitman DF, Littlejohn S Novos paradigmas. Artmed, Porto Alegre

Goria F (2008) Fraternidade e Direito. Algumas reflexões. In: Caso G, et al (Org.) Direito e Fraternidade: ensaios, prática forense, Cidade Nova: LTr, São Paulo

Kant I (1986) Ideias de uma história universal do ponto de vista cosmopolita. (Coleção Filosofia). Brasiliense, São Paulo

Lévinas E (2005) Entre nós: ensaios sobre a alteridade. Editora Vozes, Petrópolis
Montaigne M de (2012) Sobre a Amizade. Tinta Negra, Rio de Janeiro
Morin E, Kern AB (2005) Terra-Pátria, 5th edn. Sulina, Porto Alegre
Ortega F (2000) Para uma Política da Amizade: arendt, Derrida, Foucault. Relume Durmará, Rio de Janeiro
Ortega F (2002) Genealogias da Amizade. Coleção Políticas de Imanência. Iluminuras, São Paulo
Resta E (1996) Poteri e diritti. Giappichelli Editore, Torino
Resta E (2004) Le verità e il processo. In: Marini AM Processo e verità. Plus, Pisa
Resta E (2007) Fraternità. In: Flores M, Groppi T, Mazzeschi RP Diritti umani. Cultura dei diritti e dignità della persona nell'epoca della globalizazione. Dizionario I A-G. Unione Tipografico Editrice Torinense – UTET, Torino
Resta E (2020) O Direito Fraterno. Essere nel Mondo, Santa Cruz do Sul
Rosenberg MB (2006) Comunicação não-violenta: técnicas para aprimorar relacionamentos pessoais e profissionais. Tradução Mário Vilela. Agora, São Paulo
Schmitt C (1992) O conceito do político. Clássicos do Pensamento Político, vol 33. Vozes, Petrópolis
Spengler FM (2012) Fundamentos políticos da mediação comunitária, 1st edn. UNIJUI, Ijuí
Spengler FM (2018) Fraternidade, mediação e jurisdição: (des)encontros, 1st edn. Essere nel Mondo, Santa Cruz do Sul, vol 1. p 91
Spengler FM (2021) Mediação de conflitos—da teoria à prática, 3rd edn. Livraria do Advogado, Porto Alegre
Spengler FM, Dornelles M (2023) A advocacia colaborativa como política pública de tratamento de conflitos: a humanização do acesso à justiça à luz da fraternidade e da cooperação, 1st edn. Essere nel Mondo, Santa Cruz do Sul, vol 1. p 118
Tosi G (2009) A fraternidade é uma categoria política? In: Baggio AM O Princípio Esquecido. Cidade Nova, São Paulo
Warat LA (2004) Surfando na pororoca: o ofício do mediador, vol 3. Fundação Boiteux, Florianópolis

Articles

Spengler FM, Spengler Neto T (2022) Na comunidade e no judiciário: diferenças e similitudes entre a mediação comunitária e a mediação institucional no Brasil. Revista Jurídica (FURB) 26:1–23
Wermuth MAD, Spengler FM (2019) A lógica da amizade na comunidade fraterna como constituição do político-democrático: um diálogo entre Agamben e Derrida. Pensar—Revista de Ciências Jurídicas 24:1–14

Chapter 4
Community and Communication: The Sharing of a Language Capable of Consensus?

The aim of this chapter is to discuss the community, especially regarding its origin leading to its modern conception.[1] To achieve the aforementioned objective, the guiding thread of the discussion will be the book *Communitas. Origin and destiny of the community* by Roberto Esposito (2006), whose main debate lies in the stitching together of the positions of some of the most distinguished contemporary thinkers[2] on the community, its origin, the hypotheses in which it occurs as well as its (im)possibilities of realization.

The main focus is on the analysis of the works of Hobbes (2003) and Habermas (1999) (two of the authors studied by Roberto Esposito). In the contrast of a community of fear that fostered the birth of politics and, consequently, of the State (Hobbes) and of a community originated in language whose communicative action can allow the creation of consensus and the community practice of mediation as a "common language" (Habermas).

It is in this sense that community mediation will be addressed as a practice differentiated from traditional jurisdiction precisely because its workplace is the community,[3] its operations being based on pluralism of values, the presence of diverse and alternative life systems, its purpose is to reopen interrupted communication channels, rebuild destroyed community ties (Spengler and Spengler Neto 2022).

---

[1] We could cite as some of the modern definitions of community found in newspapers, magazines, electronic media and even verbally defined by citizens: a common place for those who live under the same set of norms, who share the same cultural or historical legacy; a group of people with reciprocal relations who use common means to achieve common ends.

[2] It is interesting to mention here that Roberto Esposito debates the community, its origin and its destiny based on the arguments of Hobbes, Rousseau, Kant, Heidegger, Bataille and Habermas. However, the present text does not aim to discuss each of these authors as Esposito did, but to debate those whose arguments are most relevant to the present research: Hobbes and Habermas.

[3] Here, the reference is to a community of language, of communication and not to a community of fear, whose main objective is to obtain security—a Hobbesian view—at the expense of the subjectivity of each one.

© The Author(s), under exclusive license to Springer Nature Switzerland AG 2025

F. M. Spengler, *Community Conflict Mediation*,
https://doi.org/10.1007/978-3-032-09873-3_4

Its most important challenge is to accept difference and diversity, the dissent and disorder they generate. Its main ambition is not to propose new values, but to reestablish communication between those that each one carries with them.

Precisely because it does not work with a matrix whose main base is formality and order (here considered as state-imposed regulation), mediation is the target of harsh criticism, being pointed out as a means to foster imbalance between the conflicting parties, opening the doors for coercion and manipulation by the stronger party.[4]

Possessing its own temporal cadence, placing itself "between" the parties and acting as an instrument of social justice, mediation can organise community relations, helping the conflicting parties to deal with their problems autonomously, reducing the dependence on a third party (judge), enabling mutual understanding and consensus (Spengler and Spengler Neto 2022). The consensus is based on the fact that every community susceptible to consistency and duration presupposes, continuously, the preponderant influence of a prior system of common opinions, capable of containing the impetuous impulse of individual divergences. Without this system of prior common opinions, the social tendency is to fall into anarchy, due to the multiplicity and the clash of opinions. Thus, it should not be overlooked that the notion of consensus[5] is not limited to agreement on beliefs, values, norms and objectives, it should be used broadly to represent interdependence or interconnection of the parts of a social context.

In discussing the consensus sought by the practice of mediation, the aim is to investigate the means by which one can access a minimum consensus on: (a) community mediation practices as consensual theses for conflict resolution; (b) the limits and possibilities related to an autonomous sphere of interpersonal communicative action; (c) the structuring of possibilities for mutual understanding as a means of finding other responses to state power (jurisdiction). It is within this horizon that the text will appropriate Habermasian theory: as a means of clarifying the consensual theses about the origin of communities, since, for this thinker, the community exists because it results from a possible understanding between subjects through language, as all communication aims at seeking agreement (even if this often means the imposition of the will of one of the parties involved).

Thus, working with the theory of communicative action means seeking a replacement of practical reason with communicative reason, going beyond a solipsistic subjectivity that aims at the colonisation of the lifeworld overcome

---

[4] This criticism becomes even harsher when the object of analysis is a community in which the powers and forces are contradictory and marginal.

[5] The imprecision of the term consensus is pointed out by Horowits, which demonstrated its use by proponents of the sociological theory in various different senses, among which can be cited: (a) adjustment of social dissent; (b) agreement between the role of a behaviour and the expected role of it; (c) common beliefs, which transcend the boundaries of groups; and (d) a common view concerning the identity or congruence of disinterests (Horowitz 1962). For the construction of the present text, the conception of consensus as a means of adjusting social dissent is of most interest, notwithstanding the other aspects being mentioned.

by "desubjectification" and that goes beyond the perspectives of the traditional/state process, reaching another perspective through new procedures that enable a leap in terms of autonomy/empowerment of the parties (Spengler 2016).

In addition, the discussion will focus on heterogeneity and difference within the legal reality, indicating efficient communication and mediation channels between Law and the community; freeing itself from the temptations to dogmatically establish the decision-making criteria that should be followed in legal practice; providing Law with a procedure that can account for social complexity, creating other possibilities for the resolution of conflicts.

In the same vein, political consensus will be examined from the perspective of classical contractualism, which presupposes unanimous agreement around the social contract, which constitutes as its first effect the political body itself. In these terms, the analysis will be conducted through specific points that pertain to the "induced" consensus of the Hobbesian view as a means of adjusting social dissent starting from the State as the holder of the monopoly of legal violence, in whose scenario the consequent "normative participation" of the citizen occurs. Simultaneously, mediation practices will be addressed as a strategy to achieve consensus among community actors through their "consensual participation".

To initiate the discussion, the community will be addressed in etymological terms. This discussion will be guided especially by the text of Esposito whose Hobbesian analysis on the creation of the political is extremely pertinent to the debate (2006).

4.1 *Communitas* X *Immunitas:* The *Munus* of Sacrifice and the Benefit of Exemption in the Creation of the Political

For Roberto Esposito (2006, p. VII), the community is not translatable in the philosophical-political lexicon in any other way except at the cost of an unsustainable distortion—perhaps perversion—of which our century has had a tragic experience. But even this reduction to an "object" of philosophical-political discourse links the community to a conceptual language that disturbs it at the very moment it tries to name it: that of the individual *and* the totality, of identity *and* particularity, of origin *and* the end. Or simply of the *subject* with all its most irrevocable metaphysical connotations of unity, certainty, interiority.

Along the same line of reasoning, political philosophy also tends to think of the community as a "wider subjectivity". This is because it is assumed that the community is a "property of the subjects who come together" (Esposito 2006, p. VIII). In this way, the community is linked to the semantics of the own, of mine, of what belongs to me and to which I also belong.

The community would, in this conception, be that to which I am connected and that which connects me to other people. Similarly, it is also that which swallows me, making me "just one more", which makes my identity indistinct once it includes me in the same space in which others are also included and this often can mean losing subjectivity, individuality and autonomy.

It is in this way of thinking and naming the community that we can perceive that it contains a paradox. This is because thinking communally or in community means thinking about something common in the sense of something that unites in a single identity the property of each of its members. They are owners of their community. However, the etymology of the term *communitas* and its corresponding adjective *communis*—is precisely that which assumes the sense of opposition to "own". Thus:

> In all the neo-Latin languages, but not only, 'common' (commun, comun, common, kommun) is what is not one's own; it begins where the own ends. [. . .] It is what pertains to more than one, to many or to all – and therefore that is 'public' in opposition to 'private', or 'general' (but also 'collective') in contrast with 'particular'. (Esposito 2006, p. X)

However, to this first meaning of community is joined the Greek meaning of *koinos* which is added to another meaning: *munus*, composed of the root "* *mei*— and the suffix—*nes*, which indicates a 'social' characterisation" (Esposito 2006, p. X). However, these terms oscillate between three meanings that, in the juxtaposition between the public and the private, work with another conceptual area that leads back to the idea of "duty". These three meanings are *onus*, *officium*, and *donum*. Thus:

> In truth, if for the first two the meaning of 'duty'– hence 'obligation', 'office', 'charge', 'employment', 'position' – is immediately evident, for the third it appears at first sight more problematic. In what Would a gift not be a duty? On the contrary, does it not present itself as something spontaneous and therefore eminently optional? (Esposito 2006, p. XI)

In this sense, it is important to investigate the duty (or obligation) in relation to the *munus*, which is also part of the community (hence *communitas,* or *with munus*). This is because once someone has accepted a *munus,* they are obliged to reciprocate in goods or service. Hence it is said that the *munus* is inexorably compelling since what is given has this destiny because "one *must* give and *cannot not* give". Moreover, the *munus* only indicates what is given, not what is received. It indicates the obligation that is contracted in confrontations with the other and that requires an appropriate discharge. In summary, what is emphasised in the *munus* is the reciprocity or mutuality that commits individuals to each other, as Roberto Esposito (2006, p. XII) would have it, in a mutual oath, a common oath "*to swear community* or *communion* in the sacred bond of the *conspiracy* (Esposito 2006, p. XII).

Projecting the current discussion onto the collective noun of *communitas*, one might ask: what do community members have in common? Is it truly something positive? A good? A substance? An interest? Dictionaries provide a somewhat precise answer: the meaning of *communis* should be "one who shares a burden". Thus, *communitas* is the union of people bound not by "property", but by a duty or a debt.

For Esposito, here lies the most important characteristic of the public/private duality: that is, the one that contrasts *communitas* and *immunitas*:

> if *communis* is the one who is obliged to perform a duty - or to bestow a grace - on the contrary *immunis is said to be one who performs no duty*, and can therefore remain *ungrateful*. He can preserve his substance intact through a *vacation of numbers*. While the *communistas* is bound to the sacrifice of compensation, the *immunitas* implies the benefit of the *dispensation*. (Esposito 2006, p. VII)

Precisely for this reason, the *munus* that the community shares is not a property or a sense of belonging, it is not a possession. On the contrary, it is a debt, a commitment, a donation. The subjects of a community are united by a duty (in the sense that someone says: *I owe you* something, but not *you owe me* something) that does not make them completely masters of "themselves".[6] On the contrary, it expropriates them, in part or in whole, of their initial, primary and most important property: their subjectivity.

Thus, life "in common" means replacing subjectivity with collectivity; it means accepting the *munus*, translated as the duty to share a debt, the duty to sacrifice something for the common good. Sacrificing individuality for the sake of the community and freedom for the sake of the security that only the latter can offer.

In the meantime, it is important to mention Hobbes' concept of freedom, which stated: "by FREEDOM is understood, according to the proper signification of the word, the absence of external impediments, impediments which often take away part of the power that each one has to do what remains, according to what his judgement and reason dictate". (Hobbes 2003, p. 112). It is important to note that Hobbes (2003, p. 112) mentions "external impediments" that prevent individuals from doing what they deem fit or correct. Such external impediments can be recognised in the rules of a common life, of a common *munus*, of a duty and of a sacrifice to which all are obliged.

In the Hobbesian conception, all these common duties arise from the need for security, even if achieving it requires curtailing individual freedom. For Hobbes, fear is the driving force behind the creation of the political and the birth of the State, whose main goal is to protect the citizen since the "[. . .] condition of man is a condition of war of all against all [. . .]. (Hobbes 2003, p. 112)

In this regard, Esposito (2006, p. 10) concludes that what men have in common, according to the Hobbesian conception, is the ability to kill and correspondingly, to be killed. A vulnerability so widespread that it becomes a link between individuals united by the mutual desire to murder each other.[7] Thus, life (the primary

---

[6] On the founding debt of the community, it is important to revisit some arguments by Eligio Resta: (a) debito infinito per essere stati fondatori della stirpe nata attraverso opere e sacrifici degli antenati; è un debito che si rinnova continuamente senza la possibilità che si estingua, anzi gli avi vanno ricompensati; (b) Concetto della *redenzione* (rede emere). Ogni vantaggio che si è acquisito da una generazione precedente si trasforma automaticamente in debito da restituire, è un dono avvelenato, la doppiezza della gratuità si svela. La gratuità non è gratuità, è un dono avvelenato, esiste un sinallagma ferreo; (c) Il primo, principale, ineludibile elemento di restituzione deve riguardare l'obbedienza. Il debito non trova soluzione di continuità e si rafforzerà col sacro svelato dal timore per quello che consegue dal tradimento della stirpe e da quello che questo tradimento minaccia (potestas vitae atque mortis) (Resta 1997, specially Chapter 1- Generazione).

[7] In summary, the largest community to which we belong is death. This, the moment it becomes a certainty without a set time, includes and excludes the citizen who, to avoid it, seeks security,

necessity) can be secured by accumulating power[8] (the primary passion). This is the Hobbesian interpretation of the dark underbelly of the community. In this way, Hobbes (2003) interprets the inscrutable community law: the community carries within it a gift of death.[9]

In this context, another Hobbesian paradox emerges: the relationship that binds men is not between friend and enemy, but between enemy and enemy. Thus, all friendship is instrumental in the sense that friendships are good when they are useful in managing the only possible social bond in the Hobbesian conception: enmity.

Therefore, if the relationship between men is destructive, the only way out of this unsustainable state of affairs is the destruction of the relationship itself. If the only humanly possible community is that of crime/death, nothing remains but the crime of the community: the drastic elimination of all types of social bonds.

This purpose is materialised with the creation of the State as both a constitutive and dissociative act, that is, the State "desocialises" the community bond by taking on the task of making this "social connection" from institutionalised force (Esposito 2006, p. 15). Thus, it creates a new form of community, composed of "units without relationship, suppression of the *cum*" (Esposito 2006, p. 15). It is precisely at this moment that the subjects of the state figure cease to have anything in common: everything is separated between "mine" and "yours", a division without sharing occurs.

It is precisely this relationship that immunises everyone from the risk of death contained in the community according to the contrasting opposition between *immunitas* and *communitas* that organises the current project of modernity.

Hence the idea of a *community of death*. This is the authentic community, according to Bataille (1978). But why must the community, to be truly such, necessarily be a community of death? Because death is unrepresentable par excellence. But isn't the experience of death what puts us in communication with what we *are not*, or with our *impropriety* ? Death is the lack of ourselves, it is what

trying to ensure, in every way, their survival even if for this they need to sacrifice their freedom or their rights.

[8] Here it is important to differentiate the terms "power" and "force". Thus, "force (Gewalt), is usually associated with the idea of something that is close and present. It is more coercive and immediate than power (Macht). It is spoken of, emphasising it, as physical force. Power, in its deepest and most primal stages, is rather force. A prey is captured by force, and by force brought to the mouth. Given more time, force transforms into power ... Power is more universal and more broad; it *contains* much more, and is no longer so dynamic. It is more ceremonious and even has a degree of patience. The very word *Macht* derives from an ancient Gothic root—*magan*, meaning 'power, ability'—, and has no kinship with the verb *machen* (to make)" (Canetti 1995. p. 281).

[9] One must not lose sight of the fascination that death exerts on man, to the point of having been dissected in the most diverse areas of knowledge, including in literature. On the debate it is important to read Simone de Beauvoir in the work "All Men Are Mortal". In it, the author demonstrates the need to understand human finiteness and paradoxically the fear and the need for death that we all possess. (Beauvoir 1960).

separates us from ourselves: it is "what puts us in communication with what we *are not*: with our other and with the other of us". Therefore, the experience of death is an experience of dispossession of ourselves. Death is never *mine*: it is the lack of what I possess. No one can live their own death, death is always of the other. But not even the other owns and lives *their* death. Death is essentially an *impropriety* that levels us all. And this is the secret of the community: the "sharing of the impossibility of dying *one's own* death". The experience of death—understood as "abandonment of each identity not to a common identity, but to a common absence of identity"—therefore equates to the experience of a community: since "death is our *common* impossibility of being what we strive to continue to be: isolated individuals" (Tarizzo 2007, pp. 47–48).

This sense of community coincides, moreover, with the etymological root of the term *communities*. As Esposito (2006, p. 49) argues in his *Introduction to Communitas*, it is indeed the *quality of nothing* (from *cum munus*, which means "void, debt, gift"). The community is now a gift of the limit, or a gift of death, in the sense that it is *death itself* that *gifts* the community (the community, and being-in-common, of the donors who co-share the same gift: the same *impropriety*).

It is an irremediable and unavoidable separation that puts an end to the *munus* originally characterised the social relationship prior to the contract. Therefore, the contract is the very negation of the gift in the sense that

> the transition from the community level of gratitude – unsustainable, according to Hobbes, for the 'modern' man – to that of a law removed from any form of *munus*. It is rather destructive of the figure of the *communitas*. This dissolving power corresponds to the sovereign exchange between protection and obedience: preserving individuals through the annihilation of their relationship (Esposito 2006, p. VII).

And what is released is the connection with the original dimension—Hobbes (2003, p. 115) says "natural"—of living together through the institution of another artificial origin coinciding with the figure, legally "privatistic" and logically "privative" of the contract. Hobbes (2003, p. 115) perfectly captures its immunising power in confrontations of the preceding situation by defining the status precisely by opposition to the gift: the contract is above all that which *is not* given, absence of *munus*, neutralisation of its poisonous fruits. Consequently, while in *communitas* we have the sacrifice linked to compensation, in *immunitas* we have the benefit of the exemption from obligation and the consequent non-existence of ties.

> Naturally, the Hobbesian immunity option, and more generally modern, does not occur without costs. And indeed it has a terrible price. What is cut, and expelled, in the sovereign decision is the very content of the new form, as is inevitable given the homeopathic character of the remedy put into action: filling the void of the *munus* – the original flaw – with an even more radical void. Emptying the danger of the *cum* by definitively eliminating it. And indeed the Leviathan State coincides with the dissociation of every community bond. With the abolition of any social relationship foreign to the vertical exchange protection-obedience. Naked relationship of non-relation. If the community involves crime, the only possibility of individual survival lies in the crime of the community. (Esposito 2006, p. VII)

This is because if the relationships between individuals carry conflict and a common mortal danger the only hypothesis to escape this prediction is the suppression of the direct relationship between individuals (*communitas*) using the figure of a third party that is placed superior to these people and their wills (the State) guaranteeing an indirect, but safe relationship (*immunitas*).

It is in this line of reasoning that the Hobbesian vision places us again and once more before the difference between *communitas* and *immunitas*. The 'immune' is not simply different from the 'community' but rather its opposite—the one that empties it to the complete extinction not of its effects, but of its very assumption. Thus it is possible to see the two indissolubly linked faces of the bivalent concept of *munus*: gift and obligation, benefit and performance, conjunction and threat.

Therefore, what is sacrificed is precisely the *cum* which is the relationship between men, and therefore, in any case, the men themselves. These are paradoxically sacrificed for their survival. "They live *in* and *of* the renunciation to coexist" (Esposito 2006, p. XXIII). This coincidence of conservation and sacrifice of modern life touches the apex of its own destructive power.

It is in this sense that Roberto Esposito makes an incursion into the community theory of Rousseau (1972), which he considers a myth, leading to Kant (1990) whose conception is the one who, more than any other, manages to grasp the scope and limit exposed in the field of determination of the community under the anthropological plan of the transcendental will of the law. Kant (1990) grasps the *amphibological* character of the *communitas*: its being a gift that does not belong to the subject; which rather, reduces and hollows it out by the inexhaustible duty which prescribes what it forbids and forbids what it prescribes.

Along this same tortuous path Heidegger (1989) makes a reading that recovers and values the problematic charge in confrontations of subjectivity: neither the law is absolutised as the ultimate origin, because it is its turn preceded by a 'lawless' even more original which is that *cum* to which we always belong as temporal existence: *coexistence*.

The limit puts into *communication* what it divides, thus expressing the division as a *co*-division. And this is exactly the meaning of the *community*: the communication (and coexistence) of what is co-shared by one side and the other of the boundary. In this precise sense, the representation of the unrepresentable is then a community or a communication *between* the representation and the unrepresentable—*united by the same boundary*. And the logic of the boundary can, therefore, be defined as a logic of the community (Tarizzo 2007, pp. 46–47).

Finally, Esposito (2006) arrives at Habermas (2001) and his theory of communicative action, whose central point is closely linked to the community and mediation. This is because mediation is a way of managing and resolving conflicts that works with co-sharing, which aims for the common—not in an original sense of the community (or at least in the sense that we lend it)—but in the sense of a community communication, of a "common action", reciprocal, that escapes from state immunisation for the purpose of ensuring a communion in conflict and in its resolution.

To discuss communication as a means of allowing the community and community mediation to occur, the following item unfolds.

4.2 The Community and Its Communicative Action: Common Language as a Means of Interactive Expression

Community mediation is a way of establishing communication broken between the parties due to the antagonistic position instituted by the litigation and the expectation of a third party (the State) to resolve it. Being a communicative exchange in which the conflicting parties stipulate what each one is responsible for in dealing with the conflict in question, community mediation facilitates the expression of dissent by defining a vehicle that can manage disagreement and reach a communicative consensus.

Indeed, the main challenge that community mediation faces is not to generate warm and cosy relationships, conflict-free communities or a harmonious world order. Instead, considering the endemic nature of conflict, perhaps its main challenge is to find mechanisms that enable a communicatively peaceful coexistence (Spengler 2016). Aiming to investigate how these interactions occur and how community mediation appropriates them to re-establish communication between the parties generating consensus, is why the Habermasian theory will be visited (Habermas 2001).

In summary, the theory of communicative action is not a metatheory, but the principle of a theory of the community that underpins a social critique, enabling interdisciplinary studies. Seeking a rationality[10] that could account for social complexity, Habermas leads the theory of communicative action starting from a community articulated on two levels: the paradigms of the lifeworld and the system.

The Habermasian "lifeworld" is the "backdrop" in which community actors operate and which is analytically differentiated: (a) it can first be seen as an objective world—as a set of all entities about which true statements can be produced (Habermas 2002, pp. 39–40); (b) the social world—as a set of all legitimately regulated interpersonal relationships; (c) and finally, the subjective world—seen as the totality of the speaker's experiences, to which he has privileged access (Habermas 1999).

It is in this shared lifeworld that subjects capable of language and action must be able to "relate to something" in the objective world, when they want to understand each other "about something" in communication, or achieve "something" in practical relations. In order to relate with something (people and objects), they must—each on their own, but in agreement with all others—start from a pragmatic assumption. They assume "the world" as the totality of existing objects that can be judged or treated (Habermas 2002, p. 39).

In these terms, the contexts of the lifeworld and the linguistic practices in which socialised subjects "have always" found themselves, reveal the perspective of

[10] Juan Carlos Velascos Arroyo emphasises that the notion of rationality is not presented as an empirical or descriptive concept, but prescriptive. It operates through deliberation, argumentation and critique (Arroyo 2000).

traditions and customs that institute meanings. Those belonging to a local language community experience everything that happens in the world in the light of a habitual "grammatical" pre-understanding, not with neutral objects. Thus, the retrospective relationship of the objectivity of the world with the intersubjectivity of understanding among communication participants, assumed in action and speech, clarifies the linguistic mediations of worldly referents. The facts, which *I affirm* about an object, in front of others who can contradict them, are *defended* and, where applicable, *justified*. The need for particular interpretation results in that we also cannot abstract from its world-revealing character, through a descriptive use of language" (Habermas 2002, p. 46).

Access to knowledge of something is seen as a community practice, stabilised in prior consensuses. This production of meaning takes place in a specific form of life, that is, in a community that shares expectations, beliefs and consensuses historically entwined. The set of activities and speech actions is constituted by the preliminary consensus in a form of life shared intersubjectively or by the pre-understanding of a common practice regulated by institutions and customs. Learning to master a language, or learning how to understand expressions in a language, requires us to practice a certain way of life. This, in turn, preliminarily regulates the use of words and propositions in a network of possible end placements and possible actions (Habermas 1990, p. 112).

People share experiences inherited from tradition and consensuses founded or traditional, because they have not yet been criticised—thus, they share a way of life, needing the coordinating capacities of action present in language. Daily interactions form a backdrop which, at the same time, reproduces knowledge and enables it. In this way, consciousness as a condition of access to the world loses its primacy to language.

The assumptions of a communicative action, as conditions of access to the world of life and means of forming consensuses, can be summarised in the need for participants to have mutual ability to account for their actions, taking responsibility for them; participants must be mutually willing to understand and act on a consensus, that is, seeking an agreement (Habermas 1990, pp. 208–209).

Thus, the discussion is centred on communicative action, more specifically on "consensual interaction", in which participants share a tradition and their orientation is normatively integrated in such a way that they start from the same definition of the situation and do not disagree about the validity claims they mutually present.

Based on the validity of discourse, Habermas (2001) distinguishes the following types of action: (a) communicative action versus strategic action; (b) understanding-oriented action versus consensual action; (c) action versus discourse; (d) manipulative action versus systematically distorted communication. In this context, the Habermasian social action thus broken down will serve as a theoretical basis for the analysis of communicative linguistic interactions, assessing the possibility of forming a consensus arising from these interactions.

Transferring such analysis to community mediation as a consensual practice of communicative restructuring, the two types of interaction (communicative and strategic) can be distinguished from each other, according to their respective mechanisms of action coordination or whether they make use of it as a source of social integration. The first case refers to strategic action and, the second, to communicative action. In the latter (in which we find mediation), the consensual force of the linguistic processes to achieve understanding, that is, the binding energies of language itself—becomes effective for the coordination of actions. On the contrary, in the first, the coordinating effect remains dependent on influence—working through non-linguistic activities—, exercised by agents not only on the action situation, but also on each other. From the point of view of both the speaker and the listener, the agreement cannot be imposed from the outside, either by direct intervention in the action situation or by indirect exercise of influence on the propositional attitudes of the opponent. That which manifestly results from a compliance or threat, suggestion or deceit, etc, cannot be intersubjectively considered an agreement, as an intervention of this type violates the conditions under which illocutionary forces awaken convictions and originate "bonds" (Habermas 1996, p. 110).

For communicative action to occur, it must satisfy quite rigorous conditions: the participating agents try to adapt their respective plans cooperatively, within the horizon of a shared world of life and based on common interpretations of the situation. In addition, they are prepared for their objectives in the functions of speakers and listeners through the process of achieving understanding—that is, by unreservedly fulfilling illocutionary objectives. Achieving understanding linguistically is something that works in a way that allows participants, in interaction, to reach mutual agreement on the intended validity for their speech acts or, if necessary, take into account the disagreements that have been ascertained.

Thus, communicative action is distinguished from strategic action in the following aspect: the successful coordination of action does not rest on the purposed rationality of the respective specific action plans, but rather on the rationally motivating power of the fulfilment of the deeds of achieving understanding, that is, on a rationality that manifests itself in the conditions for a rationally motivated agreement (Habermas 1996, p. 111). Not always do discourse participants have an illocutionary posture, with the perlocutionary posture being the most common as a means of expressing power.

Evidently, the offers of speech acts can only develop a coordinating effect of action due to the fact that the binding and linking force of a speech act, simultaneously understandable and accepted by the listener, also extends to consequences of interaction that arise from the semantic content of an expression. Whoever accepts an order, feels obliged to comply with it; someone who accepts a statement believes in it and will act in accordance with it. We include the understanding and acceptance of speech acts in the group of successful illocutionary and classify as perlocutionary all objectives and effects that go beyond (Habermas 1996, pp. 111–112).

In these terms, illocutionary and perlocutionary acts serve as markers for the differentiation between communicative action—in which the participants seek illocutionary ends and the speaker's objective derives from the very meaning of what they say, seeking the listener's understanding of the content they express—and the action strategically mediated by language—when perlocutionary effects that any participant in a conversation intends to provoke in their interlocutor arise. Communicative action differs from strategic interactions because in it the participants pursue illocutionary ends with the purpose of reaching an agreement that serves as the basis for the coordination of action plans (Habermas 1996, p. 110). The coordination of communicative action takes place through the formation of consensus and strategic action by the complementarity of interest plots that can also serve as a means of coordinating action (Habermas 2001, p. 421).

This rationality in the Habermasian conception has deep relationships with the way in which subjects capable of language and action make use of linguistic knowledge. In these terms, attention is turned to the immanent rationality of communicative practice that refers to the various forms of argumentation, the ability to continue in communication and to generate consensus (Habermas 2001, p. 526). Thus, recognising the existence of communication between the world of facts and the realisation of Law, between life and the validity of the norm, are formative aspects of Habermasian thought that serve the treatment of jurisdiction. This is because communicative reason is expressed in speech oriented to understanding, having as its central point not the subject, but the linguistic medium through which interactions are concatenated and forms of life are structured, making communication possible.

The more communicative rationality expands, the greater is the possibility of coordinating actions without the use of coercion, resolving consensually conflicts that occur as a result of cognitive dissonances. Therefore, consensus depends on the intersubjective recognition of validity claims susceptible to criticism. The rationality of the participants is measured by the ability to justify their manifestations or emissions in the right situations (Crystal 2000, p. 33).

Communicative action takes place from the practice of consensus, generating commitments, in a complex social structure in which coercion, characterised by the possibility of sanction, no longer presents itself as the absolute driving element of social action in conflictual relations. In these terms, notwithstanding the importance of Law as an element of promotion/maintenance of social peace, community mediation and consequently communication, consensus and social inclusion generated by it emerge as means to manage controversies (Spengler 2016).

Working in Habermasian terms the previous statement, it is found that: (a) communicative action and strategic action are two variants of linguistically mediated interaction; (b) since Hobbes, attempts have been made repeatedly to explain how norms with claims of trans subjectively binding validity and normativity manage to develop from the positions of interest and individual gain calculations of agents who make decisions in a purposefully rational manner and who only meet by chance; (c) more promising than the attempt to renew with modern means the classical concept of instrumental order, is the introduction of a means of communication through which the information flows that guide behaviour are conducted; (d) the fact that social order should supposedly produce and reproduce itself through the process of consensus formation may, at first glance, seem trivial. However, the improbability of this idea becomes evident as soon as we remember that all agreements reached through communication depend on the assumption of "yes" or "no" positions in relation to criticisable validity claims.

Disagreements are part of the communicative medium, arising from experiences that disturb routine aspects and those taken for granted, constituting a source of contingencies. They also frustrate expectations, work contrary to habitual modes of perception, originate surprises and make us aware of certain aspects. Experiences are always new, constituting a counterweight to everything we are accustomed to. It is in this aspect that the risk of disagreement inherent in linguistic communication is absorbed, regulated and controlled in everyday practices. However, communicative action is embedded in a world of life that provides a protective cover for risks in the form of a vast background consensus. The

> explicit communication feats that are achieved by communicative agents occur on the horizon of shared and unproblematic convictions. The unrest that arises with experience and criticism clashes with - it seems - the large and imperturbable rock that projects from the depths of previously agreed interpretative patterns, loyalties and competencies (Crystal 2000, p. 127).

From this perspective, every speech act in which the speaker understands something with another person, situates the linguistic expression in relation to the speaker, the listener and the world. Thus, a communicative action takes place from illocutionary speech acts, in which one of the aspects is the interpersonal relationship, which is of paramount importance when discussing other forms of conflict resolution (such as community mediation) as a means of obtaining consensus through an interaction communicated by illocutionary acts, differentiating itself from strategic action and the perlocutionary acts contained therein. It is precisely through their speech acts that the participants in the interaction achieve feats of coordination by establishing such relationships.

Speech acts, seen as processes that operate through communicative action, are understanding, action coordination and socialisation. What enters into communicative action from the resources of the background of the world of life, flows through the gates of thematisation and enables the mastery of situations, constitutes the reserve of knowledge preserved within communicative practices. This The reserve of knowledge solidifies, along the paths of interpretation, into interpretive paradigms that are transmitted. (Habermas 1996, p. 139)

However, the community, as a symbolically structured world of life, does not develop and reproduce solely through communicative action. On the contrary, strategic interactions can only occur within the horizon of worlds of life already established elsewhere, but precisely as an alternative option in case of failure of communicative actions. They retrospectively occupy, in a way, community spaces and historical times. Thus, sequences of action can occur that are integrated not by values, norms and understanding processes, but by a reciprocal exercise of influence (market or power relations, for example). This approach, of the perlocutionary/Hobbesian type (threat, fear, etc), distances itself from that proposed by communicative interaction sought in illocutionary mediation procedures (promises, requests, etc).

The illocutionary success of a speech act is measured by the intersubjective recognition that the claim of validity raised by it encounters. It presupposes a communication situation in which the participants assume the roles of speaker/listener. This role distribution is essential for communicative rationality embodied in mutual understanding processes.

However, to understand the interpersonal relationships of communicatively socialised subjects, it is necessary to start from the classic social theory that addresses the relationship between the individual and the community. Communicatively socialised subjects would never be so without the network of institutional orders and traditions of the community and culture. The world of life is structured by cultural traditions and institutional orders no more and no less than by the identities that arise from socialisation processes. For this reason, it does not constitute an organisation to which individuals can belong as members, nor an association in which they join, nor a collective composed of individual participants. Instead, the daily communicative practices in which the world of life is centred are nourished through an interaction between cultural reproduction, social integration and socialisation, which is in turn rooted in these practices (Habermas 1996, p. 143).

Normative orders, whether they solidify in institutions or remain free as transitory contexts, are always orders of interpersonal relationships. Once again, the community and the individual constitute each other reciprocally. All processes of social integration of action contexts are simultaneously socialisation processes for the subjects capable of discourse and action formed in this process and who, for their part, and to the same extent, renew and stabilise the community as a totality of legitimately ordered interpersonal relationships. These norms would result from an order sanctioned from a communicative act born of a linguistically mediated intersubjectivity.

In these terms, without the intention of suppressing a minimum coercive system for conflict management, community mediation practices, as promoters/restorers of communication between the conflicting parties, emerge as democratic means of reorganising conflictive relations based on consensus. The debate on consensus follows.

4.3 The Participatory Consensus of Community Mediation and the Normative Consensus of Jurisdiction: Should the Community Choose?

According to Habermas, community consensus is the first link in the formation of collective will, becoming the basis for legitimisation, both in action theory and in systems theory. In these terms, to organise the community, it does so through a normative consensus previously ensured by tradition, in the form of a shared *ethos* (Habermas 2000, 2001). However, this consensus does not presuppose collective agreement, although this is the final goal, since the formation of consensus arises from an "explosive tension between facticity and validity". (Habermas 2000, 2001) Consensus means that all communication is geared towards understanding, sharing expectations, seeking agreement. From this perspective, the speaker aspires to the validity of their utterance, in the eagerness for recognition from their interlocutors who are rationally forced to take a stance, admitting or not the validity of the utterance.

However, the stabilisation resulting from consensus is unstable. The risk of dissent is compensated by community institutions, such as Law. Community orders, or communicative chains, are structured on precarious understandings, threatened by the risk of dissent, and therefore, with high social cost. Alternatives range from authoritarian circumcision to plural democratic debate that leads to Law, passing through the assumption of a strategic position, or *free rider*, the one who takes advantage of any situation. The rational motivation that rests on the power-to-say-no forms a conveyor belt of problematisation in the light of which the linguistic formation of consensus appears more as a destructive mechanism. The risk of dissent is Continually fuelled at every step by experiences that break the routine of the self-evident, they constitute a source of contingencies. "They traverse expectations, run counter to customary modes of perception, trigger surprises, bring new things to consciousness. Experiences are always *new* experiences and constitute a counterbalance to confidence" (Habermas 1990, p. 85).

The risks arising from the disruption of routine by new experiences are mitigated by the backdrop provided by consensual interactions (world of life) in which participants move through consensual convictions, acquiring resources for everyday interaction. To reveal how these consensuses are formed, Habermas (2001) turns to the problematic situation of stable consensuses that find themselves problematised. Thus, in arguments, Habermas asserts that "the strength of an argument is measured in a given context by the relevance of the reasons" (Habermas 1999, p. 37). The speaker's behaviour in argumentation demonstrates their rationality: to withdraw or behave dogmatically denotes irrationality; acceptance or rejection through arguments envisages a rational action. Community actors demonstrate in their daily lives different forms of arguments that serve as clues to the discovery of different types of speech acts and community actions.

These different means of argumentation forming consensus do not guarantee any truth or accuracy, and cannot be identified as something absolute but rather as basic for the rational recognition of value. The world of the participants can evolve and be modified. However, by interacting and exchanging experiences, the actors assume the risk of dissent. Thus, if they wish to coexist, they will need to communicatively reconstruct their world of life through new consensuses. This reconstruction, which becomes necessary from conflict/dissent, can occur through community mediation as a means of re-establishing communication.

Thus, the relational character of man gains importance for Law in Habermasian theory especially when the concern is to identify criteria that will accompany the citizen in a transforming state, pointing out the mechanisms that will serve to deal with conflicts, having as a foundation the consensus in the convergence of a conciliatory proposal. Generally, a strong consensus is prepared by a substantial amount of exchanges among the group members that accentuate the reactions and positions that conjugate. And there is no doubt that, when they gather and speak together, they highlight the dominant values among themselves and to which they are linked. In some way, the fundamental transforms and what they have in common becomes manifest, just as we see patriotism, usually dormant, awaken and command the feelings and attitudes of all (during the Olympic Games, for example, or if a political threat occurs). Immediately results a tighter bond, a firmer consent, even more extreme. The majority seeks, in this case, to approach the minority that participates, driven by a similar need. And this convergence is enough for the decision aiming at consensus to be something more than a compromise (Moscovici and Doise 1991, pp. 81–82).

However, participation may be consensual or normalised, it all depends on how it unfolds. Consensual participation unfolds in a way that maintains balance among individuals, without privileging the majority or harming the minority, which, apparently, can express themselves outside of any prescribed rule (Gramsci 1953, p. 143). It should proceed without anyone being able to restrict or stop it, even for supposed objective reasons, so that everyone can get the impression of contributing to the consensus and its renewal. The participation of all individuals is desirable so that they assimilate it and adhere to it better without being trapped by personal interests, judgments or choices, because it is expected that they understand where their interests lie, what their common representations are and feel justified by each other. The individual thus comes out of the enclosure of his particular power and accesses the collective power to participate in the choices, in the formation of the consensus that he makes and of which he assumes the consequences (Moscovici and Doise 1991, pp. 76–77).

In normalised participation, the access of community members to discussion and consensus is regulated by the existing hierarchy. They are thus distinguished by the relative competence attributed to each one, the degree to which they can involve themselves in communication and in the conclusion of an agreement. In this context, everything that raises a problem and requires a decision, whether it is a dispute or an acceptance to be realised, rises from the base to the top to be resolved. With this procedure, differences are somewhat blurred, controversies are diluted, gradually reducing the heat of debates. Thus, opportunities to participate in divisions are limited by compressing an unassimilable alternative. Under these conditions, it is evident that people are hesitant to express what they think or desire, as if they feared the hostility of their peers. And by saying nothing, they consent. For more reason, if they have a lower status or if they are part of a minority, they fear to express judgments that oppose individuals of higher status or that belong to what they suppose to be larger. They are afraid of being considered as adversaries, or they have the impression of not following the correct rules of communications, or the procedures properly conceived to create reticence to participation or to censor disagreements (Moscovici and Doise 1991, p. 78).

Consensual participation falls within the dichotomy of conflictual/consensual mechanisms used to address disputes. What is observed is that, for the resolution of conflicts, the law traditionally proposes recourse to the Judiciary, structured as a state power responsible for resolving them. Thus, state judicial systems become responsible for social pacification through the imposition of normative solutions already presented through a tiered and hierarchical normative structure.

In these terms, it is up to the Judiciary, in the event of non-compliance with normative prescriptions, to impose a solution, as it is to them that the legitimisation of law enforcement (jurisdiction) is exclusively deferred.

In these terms, mediation occurs as a communicative practice that generates consensual participation, enabling a move from stagnation to change, allowing the transition—in decision-making—from a form of normalised/normativised participation to a consensual form (Spengler and Spengler Neto 2022). In this sense, decisions aiming at consensus occur differently according to the form of participation. Consensual participation offers the possibility—to individuals without any privilege over others—to confront and pronounce themselves during a deliberation, without constraint or time limitation. The agreement reached transforms the conflict as positions transmute into alternatives related to the same goal or problem understood identically. Normativised participation, on the other hand, relates to individuals who have specific advantages according to the modality that defines the conflict, guiding deliberations to favour a hierarchy of opinions corresponding to the hierarchy of individuals and primarily obeying a legal hierarchy at the top of which is the figure of the judge, who "enforces the law".

In line with consensual participation, consensual justice emerges as a response to the dysfunction of the traditional judicial model, reviving a mode of social regulation that, although perceived as an instrument of integration, presents itself as a generally informal procedure, through which a third party seeks to promote communication and, consequently, exchanges between the parties, enabling them to confront each other, on equal terms, seeking consensus. This search for consensus occurs through the parties' appropriation of the power to deal with their conflicts.

The main differentiation that arises is between the structure of the procedures pertaining to consensual justice (ADR practices), in which a dyadic/dichotomic stance is observed that aims at the construction—by the parties involved and not by a third party—of a response to the dispute, and conventional jurisdictional practices, in which the triadic character is observed where a third party unrelated to the conflict imposes a decision based on the state's function of enforcing the law. On one hand, the state's own law enforcement, which characterises jurisdiction as a state power/function, and on the other, the elaboration/concretisation/pact/construction of the answer to the conflict that brings the parties together" (Bolzan de Morais and Spengler 2019, p. 77).

The approach of political consensus arising from the contractualism constituting the monopoly of state coercion will be the subject of analysis later.

4.4 Hobbesian Induced Consensus and the Consensus Built by the Practice of Community Mediation: Another Contractual Configuration for Politics?

Historically, consensus proceeds from contractualism, that is, from the contractualist doctrine on which social order was built as a product of a contract. From the birth of the state as an organised power, which survives the prince, which has an army to defend itself and a justice system that imposes peace among combatants, the state's origin loses its divine substrate, presenting itself with earthly credentials, among them, and primarily, the constant search for legitimisation.

In these terms, the basis of the state and political power are organised force and consent. According to Machiavelli (2007), a state is the supreme construction of human intelligence and virtue, a living structure generating order because it is, in itself, "order". Therefore, it is a means, if not an end, whose main goal is self-preservation. Thus, the state is conceived, above all, as a power structure, consensually created.

The Hobbesian conception works with the idea of a legal-political construction in which the "State is the machine of machines", the Leviathan that puts an end to a hypothetical state of nature in which men find themselves submerged in the war of all against all. The state presents itself with an artificial nature, opposed to human nature, precisely for this reason useful to guarantee man's survival, even if it costs his freedom and autonomy. The absolute power of the state, defended by Hobbes, comes from a social contract whose theoretical foundation was consensus. Based on this consensus, the sovereign state decides without asking anyone's permission (Hobbes 2003).

Consensus is important in Hobbes' work (2003) only at the constitutive moment of the civil community, when men decide and consent to put an end to their natural condition, alienating their powers to a man or an assembly of men henceforth invested with common sovereign power. Consensus manifests and exhausts itself at the constitutive moment of the state, becoming the power of the rulers exclusively coercive, founded on force, on the common fear of subjects before the Leviathan (Pasini 1975, p. 686).

However, the path taken by Hobbesian theory does not go directly from consensus to coercion, but rather on a somewhat turbulent journey, from consensus to coercion and back to consensus. Therefore, the consensus rediscovered after coercion no longer has the characteristics of spontaneity and freedom inherent in the original consensus, becoming only an "induced consensus", artificially manufactured with the development and use of appropriate techniques and strategies. (Barba 1984, p. 151) Consequently, this "induced/manipulated" consensus is also force and violence and would not scandalise Hobbes (2003) since he himself did not rule out the use of force in the pursuit of a "more subtle and penetrating political mode of coercion than fear" (Viola 1979, p. 68), a mode that today can be seen and represented in education, in hidden persuasion or in manipulation.

It is important to recognise that through manipulation quick and considerable results can be obtained compared to those that could be achieved through the threat of sanction (Barba 1984, p. 152).

Hobbes' (2003) ultimate aspiration seems to be to lead men to happy conformity, to overcome even the "common fear", "organised", to the "fear of a *common power*, the fear of the subjects before the absolute power of the sovereign", into which has transformed "the anarchic fear", the "mutual fear", among the men of the state of nature (Pasini 1975, p. 684; Barba 1984, p. 152). This is interpreted from Hobbes' statement that it is not so much a matter of constraining men to obey the laws with the use or the threat of the use of the coercive apparatus, on the contrary, they should be induced, educated to love "obedience".[11] In this sense, the decisions of the sovereign come to be seen not as impositions, but as self-determination of the citizen.

However, the full identification between the citizen and the State to which Hobbes seems to lean is only an ideal goal never perfectly achieved. Working with this logic, he proposes the "theory of authorisation" in an attempt to demonstrate in a rigorously logical and scientific way this identity. By developing the theory of authorisation, the aim is to achieve objectives precluded to the theory of consensus. Indeed, the latter is content to establish that each obligation exists by the consensus of the obliged. With the theory of authorisation, more can be obtained. It is possible to make the sovereign receive not only the consensus of the subjects, but their capacity to consent, their private conscience. The theory of authorisation thus contemplates the disappearance of the conflict between public reason and private judgement and of the coercive character of the law that "is well explained in the perspective of consensus, but not in that of authorisation", since "to authorise" means to consider as one's own the will of the sovereign (Viola 1979, p. 225).

In these terms, the theory of authorisation can be well accepted by the subject in conflicts with the sovereign, because it makes any individual dream of being similar to that man or those few men who hold the maximum power to which each person naturally aspires, because it fantastically satisfies the insuppressible human desire for dominion. Consequently, the theory of authorisation is a superb deception, a delicate device with which it is intended to induce the citizen to remain in fact excluded. However, in order for the sovereign to maintain the desired order in the most peaceful way possible, he feeds the subjects the illusion of power.

Consequently, the Hobbesian theory assumes that the coercion and violence of the State can ensure the stability of the social order. Thus, it uses the political power delegated by the subjects to achieve its objectives. But how does the

[11] This conception of obedience through education, through persuasion, a product of induced consensus, is revisited later by Max Weber, especially when he writes "*The Protestant Ethic and the Spirit of Capitalism*" (1999). Specifically in this Weberian work, man is described as an "educated" being whose religious conceptions do not allow rebellion. Thus, he works and strives to adapt his life and routine to the dictates and moral values imposed by the State and, primarily, by the Protestant moral ethic. In the same vein, Norbert Elias's work is important to read. *The Court Society, 2001 and The Civilising Process,* 1994. v. 2.

political process of legitimising power occur? The relations arising from the political community and political power translate the legitimisation of the latter into two hypotheses: either the holder of command imposes his will by force, coercing its members to acceptance (in this case forced acceptance occurs), or the holder of command receives the spontaneous acceptance of his will by the members of the community because the latter recognise the former's right to command (here the acceptance is spontaneous, that is, from common consent, which is based on the recognition of the right to command, that is, on legitimacy).[12]

Introducing the discussion on political legitimacy, Darnstädt (2005), in a controversial and strongly challenging opinion, asserts that consensus is born as the idea of "organising irresponsibility", because thanks to this method of decision-making, nothing is responsible for anything. It is a give and take that dilutes. In his opinion, the problem lies at the heart of the eternal question about the legitimacy of power and the pursuit of the general interest. One of the attempts to solve the problem was to identify the Legislative Power as the depository of the popular will and, therefore, as the guarantor of legitimacy. But the Democratic State transforms into a State of parties, which forces it to seek new "legitimacies", called to be assumed and incorporated into traditional historical structures. Thus, the decision-making mechanism becomes complicated. Precisely for this reason, Darnstädt (2005), in his works, defines consensus as a trap, a ruse.

In this way, legitimacy is related to the conformity between the set of values underlying the political order and the prevailing conception of justice and law in a given community. Thus, A legitimate political order is one that is founded on a framework of values that aligns with the dominant values in the community and, therefore, receives spontaneous acceptance. However, it is impossible to find an absolute legitimacy in which the social context, without the slightest disagreement, agrees with all the values of the political order. Nor is absolute illegitimacy possible: a power that lacks a minimum of social support automatically falls with the corresponding political order to be replaced by another with a claim to legitimacy.

However, even if legitimate for a long or short time, a political order can lose this characteristic either because the dominant values in its social body have changed and the institutionalised order has not adapted to the new situation, or because the political order ceases to function properly, proving incapable of successfully managing political conflicts and overcoming the traditional crises arising from a historical process. The opposite can also occur: a previously illegitimate political order can, over time, gain legitimacy. This latter process of legitimisation occurs frequently, as a political order is rarely born perfectly legitimate. For legitimisation to occur, it is necessary for the prevailing order to be able to function well, producing satisfactory results for the community.

[12] Legitimacy, therefore, encompasses all those attributes that clothe the political mandate in a way that produces spontaneous acceptance from the community. These attributes of the mandate are primarily linked to its origin, the objectives it achieves, and the manner in which it is exercised. These attributes form value judgements about the justice, regularity, and correctness that the mandate embodies in the political order in which it operates (Souza Júnior 2002, pp. 55–56).

Indeed, the consensus arising from the legitimacy achieved by a particular political order can be classified into two types, depending on its source. On the one hand, it can result from a broad agreement of beliefs, feelings and values already established in the community through a slow and gradual historical evolution.[13] But, if there is no community consensus, consolidated by history, in the community, what will make the political order legitimate is the strictly political work, constantly built until, perhaps over time, it may come to take root in the community as community consensus.

However, political consensus will hardly manage to obtain unanimous community support, which will tend to be diffuse, as diffuse is the concentration of the community's power. In the case of political consensus supported by a community consensus, the conscious and voluntary support of the leaders of these community forces is enough to ensure its preservation. In the case of strictly political consensus, an articulation of these valid forces, in an explicit or implicit pact that supports the order, becomes a condition *sine qua non* of the consensus, and therefore, of the legitimacy of the regime. (Souza Júnior 2002, p. 66)

Community consensus supports the classification between peaceful and conflictual communities. In the former, internal tensions do not fundamentally affect unity and community differences are resolved according to negotiation procedures, ignoring parties that challenge the legitimacy of established institutions. In peaceful communities, political consensus is embedded in the broader social context. Thus, contained within the social, the political does not become an autonomous problem. However, the vast majority of these communities' constitutions are concerned with preserving and reinforcing it as a condition of democracy. This is because the path to community consensus has always been opened by the political.

In conflictual communities, the diversity of representations that members make of the desirable order is so great that it tends to threaten the cohesion of the whole. Tensions are not just the normal reflection of the opposition of interests or beliefs: they challenge the very legitimacy of the institutions. It is in these communities that, in the absence of a community consensus, the question of political consensus expressed in a written constitution around the rules relating to the political game and certain basic principles of respect and coexistence arises, without which the competition for power, a key element of the democratic regime, will either not work or, if it does, will undermine community cohesion (Souza Júnior 2002, pp. 82–83).

Therefore, the question that arises is: what is the decisive factor in the construction of the community order? Consensus or coercion? From Hobbes (2003), we observe that consensus can be induced and carry within it fear, now not of other men, but of state sanction in case of non-compliance with laws.

However, political consensus only gains autonomy for legal regulation when it is detached from a community consensus, which occurs factually in those concrete

[13] This is the consensus termed "social" by Burdeau, characteristic of what he calls "pacified communities" (Burdeau 1966, p. 18 et seq.).

historical-community realities in which there is no *civic culture* with its corresponding community consensus. The task of the jurist, therefore, is to focus on the conflictual reality of the community, without questioning its functionality or not. Their role is to find suitable institutional formulas to enable the democratic resolution of the conflict, without the pretension of resolving it (which is known to rarely happen) but rather to manage it, primarily concerned with offering viable hypotheses for this.

These institutional formulas for conflict resolution, agreed upon, more democratic and, consequently, less coercive (among which, and primarily, community mediation is seen), are difficult topics for discussion incorporated by the State in which the relations between law and community consensus develop (Spengler 2012). For such relations to be established, "filters" have been instituted which, fortunately, have endowed both consensus and the norm with a mutually relative autonomy. This filter is the legitimisation that, through legality, imposes respect for the law by linking powers and limiting arbitrariness (Resta 1996, p. 281).

This same law that is (initially and in a Hobbesian version) created to "resolve" conflicts, possessing, for this purpose, legitimacy derived from the consensus of all citizens, often fails to achieve its objectives and on other occasions becomes a factor generating new conflictuality. In view of this, it is observed that the current model of jurisdiction is in crisis, promoting the growth and highlighting the importance of other methods of conflict resolution that propose to build/strengthen formulas privileging consensus.

In this expanded horizon of transformations, readjustments and repercussions, consensus emerges as the great articulator of these new practices, being observed occupying a place in various aspects of the legal order and promoting the (re) introduction of practices that, although known, many of them, legally, did not have the recognition/acceptance of legal practitioners. Along the same lines, there is no doubt that these questions should be projected within a broad debate involving the political-institutional definitions of the Contemporary State, since it involves the redefinition of one of the basic functions of state activity: conflict resolution (Bolzan de Morais and Spengler 2019).

Discussing the exhaustion of the current model of jurisdictional provision in conflict resolution and its need for transformation/readjustment, it becomes possible to measure how the introduction of alternative practices (ADR)—among them community mediation—relates to consensus and why they are called democratic. Peaceful and regulated political coexistence is based on the recognition of the factual need for social consent. The same happens with conflict resolution. Such an endeavour takes place through institutions capable of opening spaces for compromise, which are born as a strategy that democracy offers to tyranny, violence and terror. Democratic practices of conflict resolution depend, essentially, on social adherence. The management and resolution of a conflict will only be considered democratic if the concrete arrangements that shape it, in addition to meeting the objective requirements of the "democratic model", are accepted by the conflicting parties as such.

The current model of jurisdiction—often authoritarian—, having fear as a principle, repels consensus. Compromise means negotiated composition of disagreements. The very rules of the democratic game involve a continuous work of composing demands and interests that can occur through negotiation. In negotiated order jurisdictional systems, the parties maintain from the beginning to the end the control over the process and its outcome. However, in it, the legal/state law does not disappear, it transforms into a more flexible model, adapted to concrete situations (Zagrebelsky 2005).

Consequently, a consensual community, in which part of the state legal dirigisme would decrease (showing that the State is not the only guarantor of social peace), would constitute a very favourable ground for negotiated order. However, for consensus to be achieved, more than good intentions are needed. A certain balance in the socioeconomic relations of the conflicting parties and equality of rights among people, as well as the judicial protection due to them, are necessary. From this it follows that democracy backed by consensus is, above all, an institutional construction, that is, a set of legally established institutions organised according to certain arrangements, among them, mediation.

References

Books

Arroyo JCV (2000) La teoría discursiva del derecho. Boletim Oficial del Estado, Madrid
Barba V (1984) "Opinione" e "consenso" in Hobbes. In: Dini V Soggetti e potere. Un dibattito su società civile e crisi della politica. Bibliopolis, Napoli
Bataille G (1978) La esperienzia interiore. Laterza, Bari
Beauvoir S (1960) Todos os homens são mortais. Difusão Europeia do Livro, São Paulo
Burdeau G (1966) Traitè de science politique. Librarie Générale, Paris
Canetti E (1995) Massa e Poder. Companhia das Letras, São Paulo
Crystal D (2000) Dicionário de linguística e fonética. Jorge Zahar, Rio de Janeiro
Darnstädt T (2005) La trampa del consenso. Editorial Trotta, Madrid
de Morais JLB, Spengler FM (2019) Mediação e arbitragem: alternativas à jurisdição, 4th edn. Livraria do Advogado, Porto Alegre
Esposito R (2006) Communitas. Origine e destino della comunità. Enaudi, Torino
Gramsci A (1953) Note sul Machiavelli. Einaudi, Milano
Habermas J (1990) Pensamento Pós-Metafísico. Tempo Brasileiro, Rio de Janeiro
Habermas J 70 (1996) Racionalidade e comunicação. Edições, Lisboa
Habermas J (1999) Teoría de la Acción Comunicativa, Vol 1. Taurus, Madrid
Habermas J (2000) Facticidad y validez: sobre el derecho el Estado democrático de derecho en términos de teoría del discurso, 2nd edn. Trotta, Madrid
Habermas J (2001) Teoría de la acción comunicativa: complementos y estudios previos, 5th edn. Vol 1 e Vol 2. Taurus, Madrid
Habermas J (2002) Agir Comunicativo e Razão Destranscendentalizada. Tempo Brasileiro, São Paulo
Heidegger M (1989) La questione della cosa. Vitiello V (ed). Guida Editore, Napoli
Hobbes T (2003) Leviatã ou a matéria, forma e poder de uma república eclesiástica e civil. Martins Fontes, São Paulo

Horowitz IL (1962) Consensus, conflict and cooperation: a sociological inventory. Soc Forces n.41dez
Kant I (1990) Che cosa significa orientarsi nel pensiero. Desideri F Questione di confine, Genova
Machiavel (2007) O Príncipe. Sílabo, Lisboa
Moscovici S, Doise W (1991) Dissensões e consenso: uma teoria geral das decisões colectivas. Livros Horizonte, Lisboa
Resta E (1996) Poteri e diritti. Giappichelli Editore, Torino
Resta E (1997) Le stelle e le masserizie. Paradigmi dell'osservatore. Roma-Bari, Laterza
Rousseau JJ (1972) Del contratto sociale. Rossi P Opere, Firenze
Souza Júnior CS (2002) Consenso e democracia constitucional. Sagra Luzzatto, Porto alegre
Spengler FM (2012) Fundamentos políticos da mediação comunitária, 1st edn. UNIJUI, Ijuí
Spengler FM (2016) Da jurisdição à mediação: por uma outra cultura no tratamento dos conflitos, 2ªnd edn. UNIJUÍ, Ijuí
Tarizzo D(2007) Filósofos em comunidade. Nancy, Espósito, Agamben. Paiva R (Org.). O Retorno da Comunidade. Os Novos Caminhos do Social, Mauad X, Rio de Janeiro
Viola F (1979) Behemoth o Leviathan? Diritto e obbligo nel pensiero di Hobbes. Giuffrè, Milano
Weber M (1999) Economia e sociedade. Fundamentos da Socilogia Compreensiva. UNB, Brasília
Zagrebelsky G (2005) El derecho dúctil. Ley, derechos, justicia. Trotta, Madrid

Articles

Pasini D (1975) "Paura reciproca" e "paura comune". Rivista internazionale della filosofia del diritto IV, serie, fascicolo 4, ottobre-dicembre
Spengler FM, Spengler Neto T (2022) Na comunidade e no judiciário: diferenças e similitudes entre a mediação comunitária e a mediação institucional no Brasil. Revista Jurídica (FURB) 26:1–23

Chapter 5
Community Mediation and the Mediator: Resolving Conflicts in a Non-State Community Space

All current social relationships experience conflicts at some point. These conflicts, due to a variety of factors, including the distribution and development of social roles, the frantic pace imposed by the globalised economy, and the ease of communication that—paradoxically—distances human beings and makes community ties artificial, have become more complex than those existing a few decades ago. Thus, it is observed that the current complexity of conflict is a contemporary feature seen in both global and local spheres.

Similarly, talking about conflict has become an inevitable commonplace, especially when it is observed that the "solid" response—which should be provided by institutions such as the Judiciary—has gradually faded, corroded by the incompatibility between complex community relations and current hegemonic strategies.

Perhaps discussions about the state's difficulties in responding to conflicts also occur because the solidity of institutions, paradigms and dogmas, hitherto established, have flowed, have become liquid. Consequently, they "do not easily maintain their form" not adhering much "to any form and are constantly ready (and prone) to change it". Precisely for this reason, it is possible to consider "fluidity" or "liquidity" as appropriate metaphors when we want to capture the nature of the present phase, which is *new*, in a way, in the history of modernity (Bauman 2001, pp. 8–9).

Therefore, taking as a starting point the current "social fluidity" and, consequently, of institutions (including the Judiciary), it is important to mention the exact notion of what is intended when discussing community justice as a means of responding to conflicts, especially those circumscribed to a certain community and the individuals who form it.

It is in this context that community mediation appears as a means of conflict resolution and as a possible response to the state's inability to provide a quantitatively and qualitatively adequate jurisdiction. Mediation, considered an art, the "art of sharing" is intended to create/reestablish/strengthen ties between individuals, restoring communication, managing and preventing conflicts (Warat 2004, p. 40).

© The Author(s), under exclusive license to Springer Nature Switzerland AG 2025

F. M. Spengler, *Community Conflict Mediation*,
https://doi.org/10.1007/978-3-032-09873-3_5

Indeed, the notion of conflict is not unanimous. Born from ancient Latin, the word conflict has as its etymological root the idea of shock, or the action of clashing, of opposing words, ideologies, values or weapons. Therefore, for there to be conflict, it is necessary, first of all, that the opposing forces be dynamic, containing within themselves the sense of action, reacting upon each other.

Conflicts can be intrapersonal, interpersonal, intracollective, intercollective and international. Whenever there is a conflict, one can question how its participants—as well as their individual characteristics (strength, means of cognition, personality, emotional state etc.) and any previous relations with each other—affect the development and progress of the process. Similarly, the environment in which the conflict occurred can influence its resolution. In addition, the intervention of a third party (a magistrate, for example) in the resolution of the conflict may, in general, offer greater chances of success?

In this case, what characteristics does this third party, including their relationship with the disputants, determine the acceptability of their intervention? What characteristics of this third party help to resolve conflicts and which ones promote impasse and endless litigation? If approached by an equal, who belongs to the same community and has values, habits and beliefs common to the disputants, can conflicts be handled more appropriately? Among equals, are the chances of autonomy and responsibility for dispute resolution real? Can community mediation provide answers to these questions?

Delving into such questions is the main objective of this chapter. Considering that community mediation works with the logic of an independent mediator, a member of this same community who aims to bring to the other residents the feeling of social inclusion. This social inclusion of the individuals forming the community can be realised through autonomy and responsibility for their choices and decisions, whether concerning actual/experienced conflicts or latent conflicts. Thus, bonds are created, strengthening the feeling of citizenship and participation in the social life of the community.

Consequently, "community mediation aims to develop among the population values, knowledge, beliefs, attitudes and behaviours conducive to the strengthening of a political-democratic culture and a culture of peace" (Sales 2004, p. 135). It seeks to emphasise the relationship between democratic values and practices and peaceful coexistence and contribute to a better understanding of respect and tolerance and to an appropriate administration of those problems that, within the community, disturb the peace.

In this way, this work addresses community mediation as an alternative mechanism for resolving conflicts, enabling the empowerment and responsibility of the disputants, which results in a autonomy that generates consensual and executable decisions.

Without the pretension of exhausting the complexity of the matter, but rather to provide a reflection to the academic community on the experiences lived in the performance of justice and community mediators, this is the text that is now presented.

5.1 The Social Contract as a "Community Act" of Subordination

When we mention a community we use a "common expression" to, most of the time, talk about "common places". However, if we were to scrutinise the meaning of the term "community" we could find traces that relate to the constitution of man as a civilised social being, especially at the moment when he—in resolving his conflicts—surpasses the limits and the yoke of self-guardianship to report to a "common" power and to a consensual obedience to this power created and maintained by force of a "social contract".

Especially in Hobbes, it is possible to discuss the social contract as a means of subjection agreed upon by men among themselves (escaping the state of nature and the war of all against all), creator of the supreme power of a ruler. This social contract consists of a "mutual transfer of prerogatives" and is based on the laws of nature, which primarily determine the pursuit of peace, enabling it to be contracted for its attainment. This contracting would guarantee security to men who would be obliged to fulfil the pacts they had celebrated. According to Hobbes, in it lies the source and origin of justice, determining that just is the fulfilment of the pact and unjust its non-compliance.

However, it should not be overlooked that the pact thus in force among the creatures was artificial, and that, to become enduring, a common power was needed that would keep them in respect and direct their actions for the benefit of all. In this context, the determination was to confer all strength and power to a man, or to an assembly that could reduce all human wills, by plurality of votes, to a single will. The Republic was thus created, which could assume three distinct forms: Monarchy, Democracy and Aristocracy.

Consequently, the social contract that gave birth to the Republic and with it Democracy determined the emergence of rules for rationalising disputes, aiming to cease violence and chaos. It emerged as a means of ensuring security and certainty to men, protecting them from others. It thus sought to avoid the original discord and transgression, losing, however, the ability to, instead of repressing the struggle of all against all, overcome it through consensual deliberation among free and autonomous men.

Thus, what the members of a political unit expect from power is that it ensures, as Hobbes (2003) proclaimed, their protection against the various threats that may shake society. More precisely, they hope not to be exposed to struggle, that is, to the arbitrary violence of one against the other and to the permanent fear inherent in the natural state. The minimum that can be gained from politics is to transform the indistinct struggle into regulated combat. One of the ways to fulfil the role of protection consists precisely in the transformation, within society, of the indistinct and confused struggle into combat thanks to the regulation of conflicts by conventions or laws (Spengler 2018). In this way, the State tends to eliminate, as far as possible, combat, replacing it with competition regulated by Law, outside of all violence. (Freund 1995, pp. 69–70)

To achieve this intent, the State takes for itself the monopoly of legitimate violence, raising itself in the right to decide disputes and calling for the possibility of appeasing violence by a system different from the religious and sacrificial, called the Judicial System (Spengler 2018). This latter differs from the former because it is not the guilty party that is looked at, but the unavenged victim, it being necessary to give her a meticulously calculated satisfaction, which will erase her desires for revenge without rekindling them again. It is not a matter of legislating about good or evil, it is not a matter of enforcing abstract justice, it is about preserving the security of the group by warding off revenge, preferably with a reconciliation based on composition or on any other that may result possible, through a meeting predisposed in such a way that violence does not recur (Girard 2005, p. 39).

Such a social contract, founder of the political, which gave powers to the State to decide conflicts through the Judiciary, was born primarily from the need for protection and certainty that force would no longer be the great driving force of the construction and maintenance of human relations. Subsequently, it also signalled the need for equalisation of these relations, a sphere in which it did not fulfil its role serving more to perpetuate and produce new inequalities instead of resolving them.

In this line Dahrendorf (1992, p. 40) explains that life chances are never equally distributed. We do not know of any society in which all men, women and children have the same prerogatives and enjoy the same provisions. We do not even know of one in which all men have the same *status*. Therefore, society is necessary: "because different people have to create common institutions to survive and improve their lives".

Modernly, the reflection of these issues has returned to the agenda. The social contract was unearthed by philosophers, economists and political theorists. The predominant "contractual" question asks what would be the minimum of government that would suffice to guarantee the law, order, in short, the cohesion community. The rediscovery of the social contract arises from the search for fundamental structures in a jungle of superstructures of many types, since it (the contract), above all, is a matter of human history. It is written and rewritten by each generation. Its enduring elements are, at most, a grammar of society. The question is not whether we should return to the eternal articles of the social contract, but how we can rewrite these articles anew to advance freedom under altered conditions (Dahrendorf 1992, pp. 41–42).

This freedom also pertains to the way of dealing with social conflicts in order to hold the community accountable for their management and resolution. In this sense, Weber (1999) formulated a diverse theory about conflictand its intrinsic power relations, working with emphasis on the distinction between legitimate and illegitimate power. The former refers to the possession of authority by some individuals who have the "ight" to be obeyed. In these terms, we speak of the authority of a *person,* of an *institution,* of a *message*, to signify that we trust them, that we welcome their opinion, their suggestion or their order, with respect, consideration, without hostility or resistance, and that we are willing to submit to them. Authority is, therefore, a relationship that must be analysed from the perspective of the one (person or institution) who issues the message or command and from the perspective of the one who receives them. (Boudon and Bourricaud 1993, p. 29.)

In this analysis, Weber (1999) distinguishes three types of authority/legitimacy of power : (a) charismatic, which is based on the personal quality of the leader, so that the governed submit to the extraordinary ability of a person whose authority is legitimised by belief in their magical powers, in their revelations, being worshipped as a hero; (b) traditional, whose basis of acceptance is rooted in the past, as is, for example, the authority of a king or the head of a tribe who is respected often by custom. Also serving as an example of traditional authority are patriarchal relations in which the father or husband is respected much more by habit than by their own personal qualities; (c) finally, legal/rational legitimacy is that in which respect is based on formal rules. Modern bureaucrats obey what the codified rules determine, since society accepts statutory law as the ultimate source of authority. According to Weber (1999), the legitimisation of a set of rules is centred on a process of rationalisation of modern society.

In this context, the Weberian definition of social connection is no longer given by the individual-society relationship, but by the relationship between rationality and form of action. The culmination of this process of rationalisation—secularisation is symbolised by the image of the "iron cage", introduced in the last pages of *The Protestant Ethic and the Spirit of Capitalism* (Weber 1981). In summary, on one side there is the anguish of the "iron cage" and, on the other, the unease for the emergence of emotive-passionate forms of action that compromise solidarity and the legitimising requirements of the "administered world". There arises the oscillation between "charisma" and "discipline", which expresses the difficulty in responding to the question of what force is capable of opposing the entropy of the innovative process produced by the bureaucratic automation of state functions. Thus, Weber completes the formalisation of the "machinal" (Hobbesian) image of power by reproducing to the extreme that dilemma between occasion and norm, *inventio* and discipline, political direction and bureaucratic-administrative machine, which has accompanied the modern concept of politics from its origins. (Marramao 1995, pp. 187–189)

As a holder of power/authority political, founded on formal/rational rules, the State monopolises not only force, but primarily legitimate force. In these terms, legitimacy is caused by social conditions and exists or not according to the transformations developed over the course of history. It should not be overlooked that the State also became legitimate due to the construction of coalitions to fight wars. The fight against the enemy thus became the crucial element of state legitimacy (Collins 2006, pp. 163–164).

It is in this sense that the founding idea of the political is that which, according to the words of Maffesoli (2009, pp. 31–32), is born from "inter-specific violence, violence between distinct entities". Here we could cite the holy war, class struggle, revenges and other conflicts of honour, in addition to other manifestations that can be included in the list of aggressions arising from and exercised, consciously, in good faith, in the name or for the benefit of the nation-state. This "constitutional hostility", according to the author, allows us to think of the political as the sum from a series of fatal needs that range from political involvement to social contrasts, without forgetting, of course, the personal enmities inherent in each society.

Consequently, Weberian political theory defines the state as an organisation that claims a monopoly on the legitimate use of force within a given territory, with its legitimacy also influenced by the international prestige it holds. Through force, the state aims to maintain social cohesion. Discussing Weber's social-rationalist view and questioning the means by which human societies maintain cohesion, Dahrendorf (1982) points to the position of a broad and meritorious school of thought that maintains that social order results from a general agreement on values, a *consensus omnium* or *volonté générale,* which carries more weight than any possible or actual difference of opinion or interest. However, he highlights that another school of thought, equally broad and meritorious, believes that cohesion and order in society are founded on force and coercion, on domination by some and subjection of others. Certainly, one approach does not entirely exclude the other. The utopian (as the author calls those who insist on cohesion by consensus) does not deny the existence of divergent interests, nor does the rationalist (who believes in cohesion by coercion and domination) ignore the existence of agreements on values upon which the establishment of force itself depends.

Following this line of reasoning, Dahrendorf (1982, p. 146) points to two (meta-) theories that can and should be identified in contemporary sociology. One of them, the *theory of societal integration*, conceives of social structure in terms of a functionally integrated system, maintained in balance by certain standardised and repetitive processes. Meanwhile, the *theory of societal coercion* sees the social structure as a form of organisation held together by coercive force and constantly extending beyond itself, in the sense of producing within itself forces that keep it in a continuous process of change. He then emphasises that a decision to accept one of these theories and reject the other is neither necessary nor desired.

From this perspective, the coercive theory of society can be reduced to a small number of basic components, although these premises imply simplifications and exaggeration in considering the issue: (a) the first of them proposes that every society is subject to processes of change; social change is ubiquitous; (b) every society exhibits dissent and conflict at every moment; social conflict is ubiquitous; (c) every element in a society contributes in some way to its disintegration and change; (d) every society is based on the coercion of some of its members by others (Dahrendorf 1982).

From the point of view of the coercive theory, it is not voluntary cooperation or general consensus, but imposed coercion that makes social organisations cohesive. In institutional terms, this means that in every social organisation, some are granted the right to control others in order to ensure effective coercion; in other words, there is a differentiated distribution of power and authority. Thus, one of the main differences between the Marxist theory of social conflict and that defended by Dahrendorf (1992) lies precisely in the premise that the differentiated distribution of authority becomes a determining factor of systematic social conflicts of a type equivalent to class conflict in the traditional sense of the term. The structural origin of such conflicts lies in the way social roles have been arranged to which expectations of domination or subjection have been conferred (Spengler 2020).

Just as role differentiation generates conflicts, it is also relevant from the point of view of the exercise of authority. The identification of authority roles with different attributions is the first task of conflict analysis, both conceptually and empirically, all subsequent steps of the analysis start from the research of power and authority distributions. The important difference between these last two lies in the fact that while power is essentially linked to the personality of individuals, authority is always associated with social positions or roles. It would be possible to explain the difference in another way by saying—as Max Weber does—that while power is a merely factual relationship, authority is a legitimate relationship of domination and subjection. In this sense, authority can be described as legitimate power (Dahrendorf 1992, p. 151 et. seq.).

Thus, authority, as legitimate power, can give rise to group conflicts, mainly because: (1) authority relations are always of superiority and subordination; (2) where there are authority relations, there is the social expectation that the superior element will exercise control, through orders, admonitions and prohibitions, over the behaviour of the subordinate element; (3) such expectations are linked to relatively permanent social positions, and not to the character of specific individuals; in these terms, they are legitimate; (4) authority, unlike power, is never a relationship of generalised control over another; (5) as authority is a legitimate relationship, disobedience of its commands can provoke sanctions, and is, in fact, one of the functions of the legal system (and, naturally, from almost-legal customs and norms) support the effective exercise of legitimate authority (Dahrendorf 1992, p. 153).

Consequently, to address conflicts arising from society, the state, as the holder of the monopoly on legitimate force, utilises the Judiciary. The judge must, therefore, resolve disputes because the social system could not withstand the perpetuation of conflict. The state's legitimacy to resolve conflicts thus arises from the social contract in which men granted a third party the right to wage war in pursuit of peace (Spengler 2020).

However, the social contract did not bring an end to conflicts, nor did it signify the extermination of self-help practices. What is currently observed is the existence of a peripheral social space that, in the absence of the state, becomes fertile ground for the emergence and development of parallel forces that, in addition to creating, impose a marginal law, most of the time undemocratic and imposed by force and coercion. The following discussion is built on this topic.

5.2 Uninstitutionalised Law and the Peripheral Social Space: The Interaction Between Conflict and Consensus in Extra-State Legal Practices

Currently, official Law presents a high degree of institutionalisation of the legal function, which has become specialised, autonomous, bureaucratic, and systematised, pointing out rigidly defined and hierarchised tasks. These characteristics result in the standardisation and impersonalisation of procedures, the lack of speed, and finally, the inefficiency in the application of the law in certain disputes. As the state and legislated law lose ground (due to their inefficiency, inapplicability, and slowness), unofficial law gains strength as a means of conflict resolution. In fact, we are witnessing a gradual abandonment of Law "as it is" to assign value to a new law, officially not legitimised (Spengler 2021b).

This new space emerges as a kind of "personalised state of exception", applied, above all, to the poorest social categories who live in subcultures completely alien to institutionalised Law, often resorting to force for conflict resolution (Capella 1998, p. 277). It is observed that the state offers instruments of coercion seen as "the set of means of violence that can be legitimately activated to impose and enforce mandatory legal determinations". The contemporary state has at its service the monopoly of legitimate violence. Supported by such a monopoly, the law of the capitalist state proceeds to the (contradictory) consolidation of class relations in society, managing social conflicts in a way to keep them within tolerable tension levels from the point of view of the political domination of class that it contradictorily reproduces.

However, this monopoly of state force is crumbling (Spengler 2021b). The state, the entity that claimed for itself the official means of coercion of a certain territory, now finds difficulties in "ordering", that is, in producing order. (Alpa 1987, p. 37 et. seq.) Before, such a task is assigned to it precisely because for its performance a hierarchical bureaucratic apparatus is necessary to gather and concentrate efforts. Increasingly, we are witnessing the proliferation of so-called unofficial rights that are born, almost always, from the state's lack of attention to the fundamental rights of the citizen. Then, "those social subjects who, through their liberating action, build a new grassroots societal culture, whose insurgent rights are the most authentic expression of the satisfaction of fundamental human needs and deficiencies, acquire legitimacy". However, the criteria that make up "the legitimacy of these new actors have certain limits: we are talking about that legitimacy that is constituted from an intentional, just and programmatic content, articulated not by any collective movements, but only by those committed to paradigmatic changes, with the plurality of forms of daily life and with the project of a self-managed, decentralised, liberated and egalitarian society." Consequently, these would be the legitimate "unofficial rights"[1] (Wolkmer 2001, pp. 323–324).

[1] Examples of these organisations and these "unofficial" rights are the communities organised to deal with their conflicts using, for this, community justices, which are the subject of discussion in this text and that will be addressed in the following items.

In parallel, one can find social movements/groups not identified with just civil and political actions, and with the interests of the exploited, marginalised and oppressed people, whose legitimacy is questioned since "not every non-state legal manifestation or every 'right' produced there can be just, valid and ethical, as an intermediate social body or any leading group can create perverse rules, aiming to meet interests contrary to the community, directly expressing the intentions of minorities identified with power, domination, ambition, exploitation and selfishness" (Wolkmer 2001, pp. 323–324). In this sense, the "absence of ethics and the 'just' value empty the legitimacy of this 'right'" (Wolkmer 2001, pp. 323–324). Thus, opportunities are not rare in which the law of the strongest prevails, that is, of the one who uses violence to enforce his code and impose his rules, arising precisely from the "imposition of the law of the strongest in the peripheral areas impregnable under the control of crime. organised and drug trafficking … which, in practice, reveals itself as a counter-law". Indeed, if we take into account the Brazilian reality, we can verify that "marginal law is the normativity self-produced in fourth-world ghettos, such as those currently in the hills of Rio de Janeiro and in the gigantic slums of São Paulo … ". (Faria and Kuntz 2002, pp. 71 and 120)

The crux of the matter may lie in the crisis of state legitimacy, a consequence of the growing fragmentation and diversification of social interests that result in the aggregation of such interests in the form of (re)constructed entities. Thus, while multiple identities submit their claims, demands, and challenges to the state, a crisis of legitimacy arises, represented precisely by the state's inability to simultaneously meet this wide range of demands. To overcome its own deficiency, the state decentralises part of its powers in favour of local and regional political institutions. This transfer stems from two converging trends: on the one hand, given the "territorial differentiation between the two institutions of the state, the identities of regional and national minorities are able to express themselves more freely at local and regional levels". On the other hand, it is observed that "national governments tend to focus on managing the challenges posed by the globalisation of wealth, communication, and power", with the major consequence of this attitude being the state's permission for the "lower echelons of government to take responsibility for relations with society, dealing with day-to-day issues, with the aim of rebuilding their legitimacy through the decentralisation of power" (Castells 1999, p. 317)

Therefore, the state's retraction and the opening of ever larger spaces fosters the emergence of non-governmental and self-sufficient entities born in local communities to which the citizen turns seeking refuge from the state's incapacity. Thus, if the state cedes/loses space, it legitimises the action of these (re)constituted entities from social or political forces (which may be religious, territorial or ethnic) and which assume state control in order to transform it into their exclusive expression. Thus, we see the existence of hollowed-out states struggling with all their might to rebuild their legitimacy and instrumentality.

The lack of state efficiency and legitimacy also leads the citizen to seek other instances of conflict resolution, alternatives to legislated law and the judiciary. The position of automatic distributor and executor of law (through its three powers), monopolised by the state, developed with the sole aim of interpreting the legal text literally, loses momentum and demands for a more creative jurisdictional activity grow; there is a clamour for a "diritto libero", a "living law", in which one can "demonstrate that the mere interpretation of the law is almost always an illusion, and that the decision is reached, and must be reached, based on concrete evaluations and not formal norms" (Marra, XXXII/2005/2–3). Therefore, this movement opposes the subjective belief of traditional jurists to the effective condition of legal work.

Regarding the use and application of unofficial law in conflict resolution, one can cite the work carried out by Santos (1988) in a slum in Rio de Janeiro, which the author titled Pasárgada. In this study, the negotiation and application of "unofficial laws" in conflict resolution were observed, always carried out by a mediator represented by the figure of the neighbourhood association president. From that research, it can be seen that the consequence of not being reached by the state is the creation of unofficial law, since "while one is on the margins of official justice, everything is negotiable" (Dezalay 1992, p. 214) However, the unofficial law developed in the slums of large Brazilian cities does not have official coercion instruments. The coercion coming from neighbourhood associations is very incipient and almost non-existent, it is much more about forms of pressure than coercion per se. However, the use of threats and violence as coercion instruments is growing, not only for dispute resolution, but as a means of domination and imposition of the law of the strongest (the drug trafficking boss, for example), in a model of marginal law (Spengler 2021b).

It is in this sense that unofficial law runs into the counterpoint of official law in which the state has the monopoly of legitimate violence, having a large-scale bureaucratic organisation, centralised and centralising; citizenship is attributed to individuals by the state of which they are nationals, so in principle there is no citizenship without nationality and vice versa; citizens are formally equal and are all equally subject to the power of the state. However, this is one of the characteristics of the functional crisis of the state: to possess the monopoly of legitimate violence, but not the monopoly of law production. On the contrary, "there is in society a plurality of legal orders, with different centres of power to support them, and different normative logics" (Bauman 2004, pp. 338–339).

This plurality of orders not legitimised by the state, whose centres of power are often unofficial, are de facto powers whose intention is not always direct opposition to state powers. However, some of these powers are political forces that, consequently, become direct competitors of the officially established powers, because, like them, they intend to impose their conception of rights and collective life on the entire community. In this way, in the life of states there has always been a conflict between de facto powers and constituted powers. But in the current democratic state, the novelty is that there is a certain legitimisation in the attribution of these powers to "which are only partially recognised as such" (Gerin 1974, p. 66)

In conclusion, it can be observed that as the presence and participation of the State in certain social/community spaces decreases, the trend is towards an increase in the organisation and application of rules created by citizens aiming to resolve conflicts. Such hypotheses offer swift solutions through informal procedures, but often impose decisions through threat and the application of violence. The problem arises in the absence of the State or the difficulty of applying official law, which often depends on a lengthy legislative procedure to be established and another, equally lengthy, to be applied. Tired of waiting, individuals often create and apply their own rules, even if they lack officiality. These are community rules, devoid of officiality, but recognised by a certain collective. But how does this collective form? What is its purpose? How can it be conceptualised? Such questions will be the subject of debate in the next section.

5.3 The Community on the Couch: The Difficult (Necessary?!) Choice Between Freedom and Security

What is, after all, a "community"? The dictionary states that it can be explained, in an objective manner and in a few lines as: "The state of what is common; parity; communion; identity [. . .] A group of citizens of a state, inhabitants of a city with socio-economic or geographical affinities." (Grau 2000, p. 250).

Often the word community is used as a synonym for "mass", "tribe" or "clan". Although it is somewhat incorrect to confuse these terms (as they portray different realities) the fact is that they all indicate a "collective togetherness" that privileges the whole more than the individual components.[2] In this sense, precursor signs such as the culture of feelings, the importance of the affective or emotional make this collectivity particularly pertinent.

In this text, which discusses community mediation, the concept of civic community developed by Putnam (2000) is particularly relevant. According to the author, the civic community has the following characteristics: civic participation, political equality, solidarity, trust, tolerance and association/cooperation. In the civic community, where the union by horizontal relations of reciprocity and cooperation is characteristic, "citizenship is primarily characterised by participation in public affairs"; thus, the self-interest of citizens is sensitive to general public needs; citizenship implies equal rights and duties for all, that is, citizens interact as equals, follow the rules of reciprocity and participate in government; citizens are helpful and relate with respect and trust, and it is, above all, this relationship of trust that allows individuals to act collectively. (Bauman 2003, pp. 101–103)

The community was originally the general context in which the individual was inserted. However, parallel to the disintegration of the State and the Community, man becomes aware that this general context has nothing communal about it, that it is not an authentic life in common, with-the-other, that it does not sustain itself in

[2] This statement can be corroborated from the reading of the previous chapter in which the authors researched make clear that the protection of the community comes at a high price: the subjectivity of each one.

personal and immediate relations between men, that this life is not built on these relations. It was a general context, but without an authentic cult of the community (Buber 2008, p. 66).

But, regardless and notwithstanding the cognitive/interpretative changes in the meaning of the word "community", without a shadow of a doubt it is good to "have a community" or "be in a community". In the opinion of Bauman (2003, pp. 7–8) "companies or society can be bad; but not the *community*. Community, we feel, is always a good thing". In this line, the author highlights that the community itself or being in a community produces a good feeling because of the meanings that the word carries. To begin with, it is a "warm", comfortable and cosy place. A place of relaxation. In the community, everyone understands each other, can trust what they hear, and be safe most of the time. There are no strangers in it.

In summary, "community" is the type of world that most of the time is, unfortunately, not within the citizen's reach—but in which he would like to live and hopes one day to possess. Thus, "community" is nowadays another name for lost paradise—but to which we eagerly hope to return, feverishly seeking the paths that may lead us there. Lost paradise or paradise still hoped for; one way or another, it is not a paradise that we inhabit nor a paradise that we know from our own experience (Bauman 2003, p. 9).

However, the biggest issue is the occurrence of another difference: that which exists between the community of our dreams and the "actual existing community": a collective that claims to be the embodied community, the realised dream, demanding unconditional loyalty and treating anything falling short of such loyalty as an act of unforgivable betrayal. The "actual existing community", if we found ourselves within its reach, would demand strict and extreme obedience in exchange for the protection, security and services it proposes, provides or promises to provide. In these terms, freedom is sacrificed in the name of "being safe", protected by the community. (Bauman 2003, pp. 9–10).

That is why alongside the "bonus" of living in a community there is a "burden" to be paid: the sacrifice of freedom, autonomy and identity. To gain security, freedom is lost. It is a matter of choice and it is made (and demanded) regardless of whether the community is the State—with its official law—or another institution—with its own rules of conduct, often marginal and not recognised by state rules.

Thus, to live according to state rules (accepted and approved by society), for example, the renunciation of self-defence and the right to revenge is transferred to the State which, based on its rules, punishes the guilty and avenges the victim. On the other hand, if adherence occurs, for example, to a community in a slum, protection often comes from the drug lord who makes his own rules and commands the population with an iron fist. He claims the right to punish the guilty and distribute justice. In both cases, freedom is sacrificed for security, the difference is that in the first we have an officialised right, socially recognised, in the second, we have a marginal right, created and recognised only in the community in which it was born and established (Spengler 2021b).

But, is this community the same as in the early days of humanity or has it transformed? After all, Buber (2008, p. 33) asks, "what purpose does the new community serve?" and the same author answers:—"itself and Life". The author goes further arguing that "the new community's purpose is the community itself".

In this sense, if the community aims for its own existence and the promotion of life, it cannot be overlooked that this community was the driving force of individualism's transformation. Thus, in the community I "think" and am "thought" and this maxim involves my integration into the habits and customs of the social life of which I am part. It is at this moment that the individual "I" makes way for the integrating (or invading?!) "we" and so-called "group" attitudes begin to gain space.

Along the same line of reasoning, political philosophy tends to also think of the community as a "wider subjectivity". This is because it is assumed that the community is a "property of the subjects who come together" (Esposito 2006, p. VIII). Thus, the community is linked to the semantics of the own, of mine, of what belongs to me and to which I also belong. However, if we spend a minute thinking about the way we think and name community we can see that it contains a paradox:

> The most paradoxical aspect of the matter is that the 'common' is identified exactly with its most evident opposite: what is common unites in a single identity the property - ethnic, territorial, spiritual - of each of its members. They have in common their own, they are owners of their common (Esposito 2006, p. VIII).

Consequently, the individual body owes its existence to the reality of the social body. From this perspective, the individual body is constructed by the social: "the gaze of the other gives me existence". (Maffesoli 2009, p. 218) Directing the discussion towards the constitution of the political, it is in the community of such individualities that its socio-anthropological foundation is seen. The solid constitution of this political body is the base to which the citizen turns every time they find the need to ritualise the organic solidarity that unites the various protagonists of social life. Whatever the legitimisation and rationalisation provided by the political, there is always within it a community core that is sought to be overcome, corrected and modified according to various perspectives and theoretical trends, but which, in reality, is indisputable.

Thus, Buber (2008, p. 39) summarises the birth and development of the communal, pointing to the fact that

> humanity, which originated in a primitive community, obscure and without beauty, and went through the increasing slavery of "society", will arrive at a new community which, unlike the first, will no longer be based on blood ties, but on ties of choice. Only in it can the ancient and eternally new dream be realised. Moreover, the instructive unity of life of primitive man that was divided and decomposed, for so long, will return under new forms at a higher level and under the light of a creative consciousness and, thus, the new community will be founded at the same time among men and in the individual.

This new community, born from the evolution of all previous ones, but mainly from the evolution of the political, is that community which regains its autonomy and, respecting the identity and individualities of each one, manages to organise, in a communal way, the management and resolution of its conflicts, whether internal or external. Therefore, the new community is the one that, to protect its participants, gives them means to find communal responses to communal problems, generating protection and security without giving up freedom. Analysing this form of Community conflict resolution is the pursued objective herein.

5.4 Community Mediation as an Effective Public Policy in Conflict Resolution

If the aim is to discuss a shared method of managing and resolving conflicts, community mediation emerges as a plausible, strong, and well-articulated hypothesis. This is because it is designed to create and strengthen bonds between individuals, resolving and preventing conflicts. This task is promoted by the community mediator, an independent person whose goal is to bring to the community a sense of social inclusion through the possibility of resolving their own conflicts. The result is the creation of bonds and the strengthening of the sense of citizenship and integration/participation in social life.

Therefore, community mediation aims to develop among the population values, knowledge, beliefs, attitudes, and behaviours conducive to the strengthening of a democratic political culture and a culture of peace. It also seeks to emphasise the relationship between democratic values and practices and peaceful coexistence, contribute to a better understanding of respect and tolerance, and to an appropriate treatment of those problems that, within the community, disturb the peace (Sales 2003, p. 135).

In this field, community mediation fulfils two functions: first, it offers a space for reflection and the search for alternatives in conflict resolution in various spheres: family, school, workplace, leisure, among others. Secondly, the individual gains something that, although it may seem secondary, assumes significant political proportions when they autonomously resolve their conflicts and start to participate more actively in the community's political life. Thus, it encourages and assists individuals to think as a group (us) and not as separate individuals (I-you). Conflict resolution is good when it is satisfactory for all. In this context, the greatest lesson is to value the common good more than individual goods or gains. Consequently, citizenship effectively occurs when the "community disputants" with the help of the mediator understand and enjoy their decision-making power, respecting and caring for social well-being (Spengler 2012).

Currently, community mediation is being carried out within peripheral neighbourhoods in some Brazilian cities.[3] It is a means of access to justice that aims to offer the possibility of raising awareness about rights, as well as the management and prevention of conflicts in a peaceful manner. Mediation in neighbourhoods

[3] One can refer here to those carried out in Taguatinga and Ceilândia, in the Federal District, among others.

strengthens and promotes the participation of community members in social life, making them responsible for others and for themselves.

It is important to note that in this context the term "public policy"[4] is defined as a government programme or *action* framework, because it consists of a set of coordinated measures, whose aim is to drive, that is, to move the machinery of government, towards achieving some public objective or, from the jurists' perspective, to realise a right (Bucci 2006, p. 14).

In these terms, Massa-Arzabe (2006, p. 60) refers to it being possible to affirm that "the use of the term public policy serves to designate not the policy of the State, but the policy of the public, of everyone". In these terms, the author refers to it as "the policy aimed at advancing the collective objectives of community improvement and social cohesion—or interdependence".

Indeed, every public policy is a form of intervention in social relations, always conditioned by the interests and expectations of the members of such relations. Therefore, it can be defined as the explicit and rational pursuit of an objective through the appropriate allocation of means that, through reasonable use, should produce positive consequences (Grau 2000, p. 26).

In the case of community mediation as a public policy, it fulfils an objective which is to deal appropriately with social conflicts by the members of the community itself. It requires the allocation of means (human resources, appropriate training, and structure) by the public administration to be implemented. In this sense, community mediation can be pointed out as a public policy since it is a "set of stable government action programmes over time, rationally shaped, implemented and evaluated, aimed at the realisation of rights and socially and legally relevant objectives". Such sets of government programmes are identified with the "distribution and redistribution of goods and positions that concretise opportunities for each person to live with dignity and exercise their rights" in order to ensure them resources and conditions for action, as well as the freedom of choice to make use of these resources Massa-Arzabe (2006, p. 63).

To achieve their objectives, public policies are formulated through a process that encompasses the entire procedure of discussion, approval, and implementation of the same. Especially in democratic systems, these processes develop in a political scenario in which various and distinct "political actors" (or "players",

---

[4] However, it is interesting to differentiate the expressions "politics" from "public policy" since the first means the "institutional ordering, according to resources of authority, of the social interests in dispute, regardless of the particular competition formulas adopted in whatever the material and ideal foundations of the concrete interests involved". Public policy is understood as the "technical-rational translations of specific solutions of the aforementioned game of interests of politics" (Reis 1989, pp. 113–114). Still in the search for differentiations between the expressions "politics" and "public policy" there is a need to analyse the polysemy of such terms. Starting with "politics" it is possible to use the English language to demonstrate the said polysemy. This language brings different expressions to designate the senses that Latin languages gather under the term politics. Designating the political sphere in opposition to a sphere of civil society, one uses *polity*, whereas *politics* refers to political activity and *policies* to public action (Muller and Surel 1998. p. 13).

specifically referring to game theory) operate.[5] Among the players participating in this "game" are official state actors and professional politicians (presidents, party leaders, legislators, judges, governors, bureaucrats), as well as private groups, unions, media, and other members of civil society. These actors interact in various "arenas", which can be formal (like the Legislative), or informal ("the street"), and can have varying degrees of transparency (Stein et al. 2007, p. 17).

Therefore, it can be stated that the formulation of public policies is based on "prior studies and an appropriate information system, defining not only the goals, but also the resources and the time horizon of the planning activity" (Silva and Melo 2000, p. 4). In the case of public policies aimed at the community, the process of their formulation should "listen" to the context in which it is embedded, seeking information for their appropriate implementation.

Furthermore, the formulation of public policies as a planning activity always takes into account the objective it intends to achieve, as well as the desired purpose. In terms of resolving social conflicts, public policies can occur parallel to the Judiciary or precede the judicial process. An example here is community mediation, which traditionally takes place before the initiation of the judicial process and, if an agreement is reached between the disputing parties, it can be judicially ratified if the aim is to produce a judicial enforcement order.

Consequently, community mediation as a public policy is an alternative that aims to do more than simply relieve the judiciary by reducing the number of cases directed at it. What is expected of it is a more suitable form of conflict management, in qualitative terms, as it will be carried out by community mediators, i.e., individuals who are familiar with the social reality and the spatial/temporal context where the conflict arose. Community mediation and its mediator is the next topic.

5.5 Mediation and the Community Mediator: The Possibility of Resolving the Conflict "At Home"

If the practice of mediation takes place in the community sphere, the consequence is the integration of strategies for reorganising/strengthening the community, especially because it enables access to information, inclusion, participation and the citizen's accountability for their choices and commitment to the place (community). It is in this sense that the choice for community mediation points to all the emancipatory potential that community life provides. Thus:

[5] Game theory fundamentally consists of defining a model of "rational" behaviour in the face of a conflict of interests or a decision-making process. Its study provides theoretical insights that demonstrate how formal mathematical analysis can facilitate group decision-making. Game theory is based on the rationalist assumption in which possibilities are established mathematically. It assumes that the objectives are defined by the participants of the game.

> The community sphere is, in itself, a space of great wealth for its ability to disseminate and apply peaceful methods of conflict management or handling differences. Mediation, as a tool suitable for this purpose, offers the protagonists - those who share the community space - the opportunity to exercise collective action in which they themselves facilitate the solution of problems that arise in their small communities. In this sense, the development of these processes, as well as the transfer of specific mediation tools and techniques to community members, constitute a valuable contribution and a concrete advance in relation to our maturity as a society and effectively collaborate towards an ideal of a more satisfying community life (Nató et al. 2006, p. 109).

It is precisely for this reason that it can be stated that community mediation has a primary role of utmost importance, which is precisely to "restore confidence to cities and suburbs, by studying their reality and potentialities" in depth. To fulfil this intention, it proposes the creation of an urban democracy, resulting from the search for new ways for "citizens to become actual citizens, to take responsibility for their city, for their suburb, to create new projects for themselves" (Six 2001, p. 171).

Such an objective can be more easily met in community mediation, as it takes place within the community itself, and the mediator is a resident of the neighbourhood who knows and shares the reality experienced by the disputing parties. In this sense, their legitimacy is based on their personal characteristics and the trust they inspire in the parties.

Community mediation is conducted by mediators who are members of the community. "It is mediation for, in and, above all, by the community". The dialogic potential in this process is ensured by the horizontal manner in which the community mediator conducts the process and also by the participation of the community as co-responsible in the celebration of mutual commitments that guarantee a future of social pacification, within diversity. There is no ongoing judicial process to delimit the parameters in which the dialogue will be established. In this sense, the reference is in the ethics of alterity and not in the authority of the law (Foley 2011).

Unlike the magistrate who has state/bureaucratic legitimisation to deal with conflicts, the community mediator has legitimacy based on their conduct and personal values, the main consequence of which is to inspire in the disputing parties the certainty that their problems are being dealt with by an equal. Thus, conflicts addressed to community mediation have the presence of a third party who knows the reality, values and habits of the disputing parties (Spengler and Martini 2020). This third party speaks the same language as the disputing parties and has legitimacy that is not granted by the State but by the parties themselves, based on their characteristics, their conduct, their code of ethics and morals.

In traditional jurisdiction, united by conflict, litigants wait for a third party to "solve" it. They wait for the Judiciary to say who has more rights, more reason or who is the winner of the dispute. This is a transfer of prerogatives that, by creating "normative walls", rigidifies the solution of the dispute in favour of legal security, ignoring that daily reinvention and the opening of new paths are inherent to a democratic treatment (Spengler 2016).

This transfer of responsibilities regarding conflict management is directed towards the judge who translates it into his own language.[6] Thus, starting from Weberian rationalisation process, the State, by holding the form of legal power, also holds the legitimate monopoly of binding decision-making. Therefore, attention remains focused on the figure of the judge, from whom the final word is expected, "no matter what, but the last". The judge's position among the disputants is a complicated matter, as he does not allow himself to be confined to the easy formula of the law that ensures a "safe distance" from the reasons of one and the other. He lives in the conflict and from the conflict he decides, pronouncing the final word (Resta 2020, p. 65).

On the other hand, the community mediator (like all mediators) does not impose a decision, but merely facilitates dialogue between the parties. From this perspective, "community justice constitutes a counter-hegemonic movement challenging the imposition of a monolithic and supposedly universal model of justice" (Foley 2011).

If the purpose of mediation is to hold the disputants accountable for handling the dispute that unites them based on an ethic of alterity, there are two basic forms of mediation to achieve this end: mandatory and voluntary. Mandatory mediation is that which arises from legal determination or from the will previously contractually defined by the parties. Voluntary mediation is that defined by the parties, by mutual agreement, upon the existence of an impasse. It cannot be imposed on either of them (Morais and Spengler 2019).

To guide the debate, it is important to note that there are two types of mediation, one that seeks its institutionalisation and another that sees mediation as an autonomous possibility. Thus, we have institutional mediation, which performs a specific task in service, at the same time, of its institution and its clients. In these terms, justice itself wanted to establish mediators who would alleviate the congestion of the courts, trying to prevent such disputes from reaching these courts, being previously and amicably regulated, under the control of a mediator. Alongside institutional mediators, there are citizen mediators. Their origin is completely different. They are not manufactured by institutions, they are "natural" mediators, who are born in social groups; they are secreted by them for the needs of communication. They do not have power as such, they are not judges who will sentence, nor arbitrators to whom the conclusion of a dispute is delegated; they have no more than moral authority. If someone turns to them, it is because they consider them to be, not gurus who decide, but, on the contrary, wise people who suggest. They open a new path in relation to the impasse in

[6] This happens, according to Blanchot (1996), because the judge has the right to be the sole *master of language*. The expression *master of language* is decisive and dense, as can be that of a thinker like Maurice Blanchot, who worked very convincingly on the power of writing and on the idea of community. The connection between language and community is not, obviously, unforeseen, but finding links and mediations through the judge opens unsuspected paths through which it is discovered that the language of the community never corresponds to the community of language.

which someone has lost themselves, to a dilemma from which they want to escape, involving themselves or others (Six 2001, pp. 28–31).

In addition to having different origins, institutional and citizen mediators also have different behaviours/ways of acting. Firstly, institutional mediators are essentially specialists trained to address a specific, well-defined problem, for which they will be held accountable. Citizen mediators, on the other hand, are citizens among citizens. And if the former are asked to bring solutions to problems because they appear to express power, the position relative to citizen mediators will be different. They are approached as equals, asked to be truly someone who will not be the arbitrator who sentences, someone who will not bring down the weight of their power, someone who will rather bring help and technical assistance. What will be asked of citizen mediators? They should be, by their presence, their welcome, their listening, someone who will allow progress in dealing with the problem that exists with another, in the family, in the company, in the neighbourhood. Thus, citizen mediators are intended to meet people, first and foremost. They do not resolve conflicts: they meet people who are in a conflict situation. Citizen mediators do not bring an external solution, but stimulate freedom, courage, self-will. Being a citizen mediator is an art that, like all arts, never ceases to be refined (Six 2001, pp. 34–35).

In these terms, citizen mediators are those who "even though they are great technicians, are above all street people, people of the trade, those who think their place within a comprehensive vision, who refuse all corporatisms and want to organise together, with everyone, a common life" (Six 2001, p. 136).

Consequently, mediation carried out in community justice projects works with the logic of "citizen mediators". This is because the mediators are members of the community itself, chosen and trained for the exercise of mediation. They are individuals who, with the aim of benefiting everyone, dedicate their time and responsibility to mediating conflicts in search of an effective social bond among the members of that community. They are volunteers, who work because they believe in their social role as mediators, who actively participate in society, and take on the task of transmitting to their peers all the knowledge that has been offered to them (Sales 2004, p. 136).

However, the fact that it takes place within the community itself, through the intervention of mediators secreted by it, does not mean that community justice has no ties with the State, referring only to an unofficial way of dealing with conflicts. Indeed, community justice that aims to generate "emancipation creates a circular chain between conflict, dialogue, solidarity, networked community and the State, under which new social practices emerge". This transition of forms The shift from traditional/bureaucratised responses to conflict towards emancipatory/solidarity alternatives weaves "new social networks in the spheres closest to life—the domestic space, the community, citizenship". This also happens with the participation of the State "stimulating initiatives and coordinating different experiences, safeguarding community autonomy, enhances the capacity for social transformation exactly where conflicts emerge" (Foley 2011).

Similarly, community mediation centres should seek communication with state or non-state institutions aimed at other purposes not necessarily mediation, in order to create a network of multiple knowledge that communicate with each other, enhancing the work and training of their mediators as agents of social transformation. Community mediation can, ultimately, contribute to the articulation between various collective agents (Foley 2011).

This is precisely why community mediation presents itself effectively as an "instrument of peace and democratic politics", all because it offers: first, "the possibility of access to Justice; second, the resolution of conflicts through dialogue and mutual understanding;" in addition, in a third moment, "the prevention of conflicts, as the parties become responsible for their decisions, and also, because they are decisions discussed and agreed based on solidarity;" furthermore "when it solves conflicts based on dialogue, it transforms them and enables new bonds between people; it makes them aware of their rights and how to seek these rights"; and finally, "it socially includes the excluded when it enables poor individuals to act as mediators or as parties, offering them the opportunity to discuss and solve their conflicts"(Sales 2003, p. 169).

In these terms, community mediation is a great step towards returning to the community the resolution of its conflicts, working mainly with what Blanchot (1996) called the *Law of Friendship*. Unfortunately, the more friendship loses its character of spontaneous glue of society, the more it needs to be prescribed by a law that contains not only ethical-religious imperatives, but strictly legal ones. When we lose friendship as the spontaneous glue of social coexistence, we start to work with the binary code of friend-enemy and therefore we arm ourselves with laws and "inspectors" of the law who "state the right" so that we can coexist.

Community justice is a different bet that is not based on codes, written/positivised rules and the power/legitimacy of the Judiciary and its magistrates. Without failing to recognise the importance of such institutions and their professionals, community justice bets on friendship as a means of guaranteeing the community autonomy and responsibility to deal with its conflicts with the help of a third party, equal, legitimised by their moral characteristics and their bonds, not institutional, but of friendship.

5.6 The Paths of Community Mediation in Practice: The Main Techniques

The purpose of this item is to point out the main mediation techniques that are available to the community mediator in the development of their role as a facilitator of communication between the conflicting parties. The techniques, also known as tools, are several and can be used throughout the entire mediation session. However, only the most used and those considered most important will be presented here.

Before the start of mediation, it is necessary to build the *rapport*, as it is the biggest factor in the acceptance of the mediator. The *rapport* refers to the degree of freedom in people's communication and the quality of human contact. It expresses the acceptance of the mediator and the trust in his work on the part of the mediating parties (Spengler 2021b).

Most of the time the bond of trust between mediator and mediating parties begins at the first contact. Within minutes, empathy arises and generates trust which will allow a peaceful mediation procedure. In these terms, the *rapport* varies according to people and can be very quick to ensure empathy and harmony of work or not. The quality in the relationship—harmony, trust, empathy—is a prerequisite for the most suitable solution (flows naturally) for the conflict.

Another important technique in community mediation is the one known as *active listening*. The certainty of its importance is due to the fact that we have a great need to be heard and to know that others care about what we say and care about listening to us. People need to say what they feel. Listening well is an important skill that can be used in a difficult dialogue (Spengler 2021a).

The best form of communication is the one that recognises the other's need to express themselves. That's why advice should be replaced by active listening in order to show that what the other says and feels is being understood and is important. Giving advice usually presents itself as a means of domination, it is a way of paternalism. Whoever advises places themselves in a superior position. Advice blocks the needs for expression, recognition and emancipation of the advised. That's why listening and *actively listening* is the best way to help the mediating parties (Vasconcelos 2008, pp. 65–66).

Active listening is the technique by which the listener seeks to understand and communicate about the meaning and reason for verbal and non-verbal messages (body posture), thus perceiving hidden information contained in communication. Consequently, it is necessary to "listen" to the non-verbal communication, observing all their body movements. A mediator who does not understand a look will not understand a lengthy explanation.

Similarly, it is necessary to "read" not just the words, but the posture, what is happening inside the other person. If the posture is not genuine, the words will not matter. The listener's posture should be one of curiosity, it should be of someone who cares about who and what they are listening to. However, "listening will only be powerful and efficient if it is authentic. Authenticity means that you are listening because you are curious and because you care, not just because you should do this" (Stone et al. 2004, pp. 100–101.)

Through this technique, the mediator assures the speaker that they are being listened to, demonstrates acceptance of emotions, allows them to explore them, clarifying what they really feel and why, as well as physiologically stimulating the release of tension, allowing them to express themselves emotionally. Active listening is, above all, listening without judgement.

One of the ways to be a good listener involves asking questions, listening carefully to what was said, recognising their points of view, being attentive and looking into the eyes of the speaker and often summarising what was heard (Spengler 2021a).

Through the *summarising technique*, the mediator presents the way in which the issues, interests and feelings were identified. Naturally, the parties will debate the content of this summary, as well as clarifications about the issues raised. During this period, everyone will discuss the information that still needs some supplement, while at the same time trying to better understand what the main issues, needs and also possibilities are (Spengler 2021a).

The application of the *summarising technique* begins immediately after the conflicting parties have spoken, when the mediator synthesises all the controversy presented so far, verifying the main issues present, as well as the underlying interests together with the parties. It is recommended not to make the *summary* immediately after only one of the people has spoken, as by doing so, the mediator may give the impression to the other party that they are endorsing the point of view presented. This *summary* is of utmost importance, as it gives direction to the mediation session and, above all, focuses the discussion on the main aspects present. For the mediator, it is an effective organisation of the session, as it establishes an impartial, neutral and prospective version of the facts identifying what the issues to be debated in the mediation are and what the real interests and needs of those involved in the conflict are (Azevedo and Bacelar 2007, p. 54).

The *summary* makes the parties realise the way and the interest with which the mediator has focused the controversy, as well as allows them to test their understanding of what was indicated.

It is worth noting that the tone of voice used when verbalising what was heard from the other is very important. When people hear us repeat what they said, they are likely to be sensitive to the slightest hint of criticism or sarcasm. Similarly, they are negatively affected by a declarative tone, which implies that we are telling them what is happening inside them.

Thus, the *summarising technique* aims not only at mutual recognition of interests and feelings, but also at humanising the conflict as a positive association and possibility of personal/social growth. In these terms, it brings the parties closer together, allowing them to reflect on their postures and understand why some solutions pointed out satisfy or do not satisfy their desires and the desires of the other party involved in the dispute (Spengler 2021a).

In addition to *active listening* and *summarising*, another working tool in mediation is *questioning*. They serve to welcome the parties, to clarify feelings, interests and issues involved in the conflict, to build a list of solution options for the agreement and to test it. Questions are traditionally constructed based on: what, when, where, how much and who (Spengler 2021a).

First, the mediator needs to listen, then *ask*. Instead of advising, they should *ask*. Appropriate questions support and complement the process of listening and recognition. *Asking* clarifies, without offending. The question protects the mediator from the rush to judge the other or from the habit of giving advice. Through the question, it is possible to assist the parties in narrating and better interpreting their own behaviour (Vasconcelos 2008, p. 66).

Finally, questions should be asked with great care. They can be of the "open" or "closed" type (Barnes 2002, p. 69 et seq. and Almeida Júnior 2005, p. 125 et seq.) The choice of one or the other form of questioning is linked to the moment of its elaboration, that is, to the "stage" at which the mediation is at. Consequently: *(a) open questions* : are those that encourage the interlocutor to develop ideas in the form of a set of sentences to answer them. That's why open questions are prioritised, they can be a source of a more detailed explanation of the conflict also serving for the construction of possible response options to it; *(b) closed questions:* closed questions allow for "yes", "no" and other very specific answers. These questions can be used to commit people and find out their positions. Moreover, they are traditionally used to check if the mediators understood the information received.

The *technique of asking* has a peculiar importance in the mediation procedure as it applies throughout the session. When well applied, this technique allows for the *identification of issues, interests and feelings*. This identification occurs for a good part of the procedure, focusing more intensely during the phase of reasons exposition by the people. At this moment, it is up to the mediator to record the controversial issues, the real interests and which feelings should eventually be debated so that the mediation reaches a good term—even if there is no agreement.

Clarifying *interests, issues and feelings* may help people to advance in the elaboration of a possible agreement, as they may perceive each other's perspectives and needs.

The chance to replace a phase of heightened emotions with one in which the conflicting parties begin to show empathy in search of a solution to their problem is what mediation can offer best. It is important to note that throughout the procedure various feelings will be manifested, and it is up to the mediator to identify them so that everyone feels adequately heard and understood (Spengler 2021a).

The biggest challenge at this moment is to structure feelings outside of the problem, since the common model is to structure the problem exclusively as a substantive disagreement. Structuring feelings outside of the problem is a way to face the doubt: is it necessary to avoid or bring up certain issues? The costs involved in sharing feelings when they come to the surface seem very high. The risk is to hurt people and/or ruin relationships. But, if feelings are at the centre of what is happening, they *are* the business and ignoring them is impossible (Stone et al. 2004, pp. 100–101.)

However, the difficulty of identifying and expressing feelings is very common especially among people and professions in which the professional code means a discouragement to these demonstrations considered as "weakness". But, expressing "vulnerability" and feelings can help to resolve conflicts. This is one of the rules of non-violent communication (Rosenberg 2006, p. 144).

If one of the mediators, during his manifestation, asked several questions to the other and—because it was in the previous phase of information gathering—did not get an answer, the mediator should write down all these questions and, when this session starts, present them to the other person.

The joint session of identifying interests, issues and feelings tends to be the most anxious stage of mediation, as it is where people let go the most.

Throughout the mediation procedure, various feelings will be manifested: resentment, hatred, frustration, envy, jealousy, fear, hurt, love ... which should be identified so that the person feels adequately heard and understood. Naturally, if the controversial issues, the interests and the feelings that need to be addressed for the mediation to evolve have been clarified, the mediator should examine the need to start individual sessions to validate feelings (Spengler 2021a).

It is always very useful to *validate feelings,* indicating to everyone that the mediator identified, in a normalising tone, the feeling generated by the conflict. The *validation of feelings* should only occur in joint sessions if the mediators share the same feeling . When *validating feelings*, the mediator should not indicate to the mediator that he is right about the merit of the dispute but that he identified his feelings that result from the conflict under examination and did not adopt a judgemental attitude. Thus, it is necessary to avoid the confusion that the *validation of feelings* is, in fact, an *agreement with feelings,* which can raise doubts about the mediator's conduct (Azevedo and Bacelar 2007, p. 59).

If he considers that there is no need to *validate feelings* so that the mediators can examine their issues objectively, the mediator should select the controversial point by which he will start the issue resolution phase. Many mediators prefer to start with simpler issues to stimulate a positive feeling that the mediation is being productive. Other mediators choose to start with issues related to communication between people—since resolving this issue adequately assists in resolving the others (Azevedo and Bacelar 2007, p. 64).

Mediation develops better if the interests and issues present in the conflict are satisfactorily captured. The issue is a controversial point. Thus, issues do not relate to personality, values and religious beliefs; they have, therefore, an objective nature.

An interest can be defined as something that the conflicting party aims to achieve or obtain. In the mediation process, the most varied interests will be presented—regardless of whether they are legally protected or not. The mediator, faced with so much information, will have to strive to reconcile interests in order to facilitate consensus. The interests are in conflict (divergence). The mediator will attempt to shift these interests from a divergent to a convergent level, for all parties involved, and thus achieve better mutual understanding, learning about better ways to resolve disputes and, as a result, reach an agreement (Azevedo and Bacelar 2007, p. 60).

The goal is to achieve a positive outcome, an outcome that protects all essential interests. A positive outcome can take various forms. One of them is an agreement that satisfies the interests of both parties in conflict (Ury 2007, p. 200).

To achieve this outcome, it is necessary to show the conflicting parties that everyone has interests in resolving the dispute and that the solution will come from them. This is because humans tend to polarise their conflicting relationships, believing that for one to succeed, the other must necessarily give up their claims/interests.

Here is where the mediator's role comes in to help *depolarise the conflict*; without any form of pressure, the mediator will show that in most cases, people's real interests are congruent and interconnected, and this was not noticed before due to communication failures.

The *technique of praise*, also known as positive reinforcement, involves the mediator giving a positive response to a praiseworthy, efficient, and positive initiative from the conflicting party or their lawyer. Thus, praise is a way to stimulate this initiative/behaviour (Spengler 2021a).

Often, the parties in mediation need to ponder before responding and therefore, usually remain in *silence*. The mediator should consider *silence* as an ally in deepening responses. It is important, in this case, to avoid asking questions or supplementing them. Brief *silence* should be considered an ally in these moments (Spengler 2021a).

This is because silence reveals one's deference to the OTHER, facilitating dialogue. In this sense, *silence* becomes a "verbal" behaviour as recommendable as all those mentioned here (Almeida Júnior 2005, p. 127). However, the presence of *silence* for very prolonged periods can arouse fears and anxieties and even "break" the rhythm of the mediation session.

In addition to *silence* as a means of "feeling" the other, the *technique of role reversal* aims to stimulate empathy among the conflicting parties by guiding each one to perceive the context also from the other person's perspective.

The parties in mediation feel embarrassed by the fact that they are in court and tend to assign blame or responsibility for being in dispute. Therefore, the *technique of role reversal* serves for each of the conflicting parties to put themselves in the other's place, perceiving the context in which they are inserted and the perspective they have of the conflict.

The *technique of identifying options* aims to formulate "exits" for the conflict in quantity, by freeing thought and stimulating the creativity of all involved. Precisely for this reason, this tool is also known as "brainstorming". To put it into practice, it is important to highlight the moment to leave the past aside and focus on how to proceed in the present so that the future becomes better.

The valid options suggested/constructed/created by the parties in mediation should be based on objective criteria (reality), which need to be examined carefully. These objective criteria relate to: economic, moral and legal values that necessarily need to be observed in decision making.

References

Books

Almeida Júnior S de (2005) Negociação: técnica e arte. Qualitymark, Rio de Janeiro

Alpa G (1987) Crisi dello Stato e sociologia del diritto. Aspetti di diritto privato. In: Treves R Crisi dello Stato e sociologia del diritto. Franco Angeli, Milano

Azevedo AG de, Bacellar RP (2007) Manual de Autocomposição Judicial. Coleção: estudos em arbitragem, mediação e negociação. André Gomma de Azevedo, Ivan Machado Barbosa (Org.). Grupos de Pesquisa, Brasília

Barnes GP (2002) Negociando com sucesso: deixando que outras pessoas o sigam, 1st edn. Amadio, São Paulo
Bauman Z (2001) Modernidade líquida. Tradução de Plínio Dentzien. Jorge Zahar, Rio de Janeiro
Bauman Z (2003) Comunidade: a busca por segurança no mundo atual. Jorge Zahar, Rio de Janeiro
Bauman Z (2004) Amor líquido—sobre a fragilidade dos laços humanos. Tradução de Carlos Alberto Medeiros. Jorge Zahar, Rio de Janeiro
Blanchot M (1996) Pour I´amitié. Fourbis, Paris
Boudon R, Bourricaud F (1993) Dicionário crítico de sociologia. Ática, São Paulo
Buber M (2008) Sobre Comunidade. Perspectiva, São Paulo
Bucci MPD (2006) O conceito de política pública em direito. In Políticas públicas: reflexões sobre o conceito jurídico. Maria Paula Dallari Bucci (organizadora). Saraiva, São Paulo
Capella JR (1998) Os cidadãos servos. Sérgio Antônio Fabris, Porto Alegre
Castells M (1999) O poder da identidade. A era da informação: economia, sociedade e cultura, 3rd edn. vol 2. Paz e Terra, São Paulo
Collins R (2006) Teorie Sociologiche. Il Mulino, Bologna
Dahrendorf R (1982) As classes e seus conflitos na sociedade industrial. Brasília: Editora Universidade de Brasília
Dahrendorf R (1992) O conflito social moderno: um ensaio sobre a política da liberdade. Jorge Zahar/Edusp, São Paulo
Dezalay Y (1992) *Marchand du Droit*: la Restructuration de l'Ordre Juridique International par les Multionationales du Droit
Esposito R (2006) Communitas. Origine e destino della comunità. Torino: Enaudi
Faria JE, Kuntz R (2002) Estado, sociedade e direito. Qual o futuro dos direitos? Estado, mercado e justiça na reestruturação capitalista. Max Limonad, São Paulo
Foley GF (2011) A justiça comunitária para a emancipação. In: Spengler FM, Lucas DC Justiça restaurativa e mediação: políticas públicas no tratamento dos conflitos sociais. UNIJUí, Ijuí
Freund J (1995) Sociología del conflicto. Ministerio de Defensa, Secretaría General Técnica. D. L, Madrid
Gerin G (1974) La crisi dello Stato Democrático. Cedam, Padova
Girard R (2005) La violenza e il sacro. Adelphi, Milano
Grau ER (2000) O direito posto e o direito pressuposto, 3rd edn. Malheiros, São Paulo
Hobbes T (2003) Leviatã ou a matéria, forma e poder de uma república eclesiástica e civil. São Paulo: Martins Fontes
Maffesoli M (2009) La trasfigurazione del político. L'efervescenza dell'immaginario postmoderno. Tradução de Rossella Rafele. Francesco Bevivino Editores SRL, Milão
Marramao G (1995) Poder e secularização. As categorias do tempo. Editora Universidade Estadual paulista, São Paulo
Massa-Arzabe PH (2006) Dimensão jurídica das políticas públicas. In: Políticas públicas: reflexões sobre o conceito jurídico. Maria Paula Dallari Bucci (org). Saraiva, São Paulo
Morais JLBde, Spengler FM (2019) Mediação e arbitragem: alternativas à jurisdição, 4th edn. Livraria do Advogado, Porto Alegre
Muller P, Surel Y (1998) L'analyse des politiques publiques. Montchestein, Paris
Nató AM, Querejazu MGR, Carbajal LM (2006) Mediación Comunitária. Conflictos en el escenario social urbano. Editorial Universidad, Buenos Aires
Putnam RD (2000) Comunidade e democracia: a experiência da Itália moderna, 2nd edn. FGV, Rio de Janeiro
Resta E (2020) O Direito Fraterno. Essere nel Mondo, Santa Cruz do Sul
Rosenberg MB (2006) Comunicação não-violenta: técnicas para aprimorar relacionamentos pessoais e profissionais. Tradução Mário Vilela. Agora, São Paulo
Sales LMdeMS (2003) Justiça e mediação de conflitos. Del Rey Editora, Belo Horizonte
Sales LMdeMS (2004) Justice and conflict mediation. Del Rey Editora, Belo Horizonte

Santos BdeS (1988) O discurso e o poder. Ensaios sobre a sociologia da retórica jurídica. Sérgio Antônio Fabris, Porto Alegre

Silva PLB, Melo MABde (2000) O processo de implementação de políticas públicas no Brasil: características determinantes de avaliação de programas e projetos. In: Cadernos de pesquisa, 48, Núcleos de Políticas Públicas—NEPP/UNICAMP

Six JF (2001) Dinâmica da mediação. Del Rey, Belo Horizonte

Spengler FM (2012) Fundamentos políticos da mediação comunitária, 1st edn. UNIJUI, Ijuí

Spengler FM (2016) Da jurisdição à mediação: por uma outra cultura no tratamento dos conflitos. 2ª edn. UNIJUÍ, Ijuí

Spengler FM (2018) Fraternidade, mediação e jurisdição: (des)encontros, 1st edn. Essere Nel Mondo, Santa Cruz do Sul, vol 1. p 91

Spengler FM (2020) Il terzo e le leggi del conflitto Un dibattito necessario, 1st edn. Edizioni Classi, Pariggi/Firenze

Spengler FM (2021a) Mediação de conflitos - da teoria à prática -, ed. 3. Porto Alegre: Livraria do Advogado

Spengler FM, Martini SR (2020) O terceiro fraterno na composição triádica dos conflitos sociais. Nomos 40(1):17–32

Stein E, Tommasi M, Echebarría K, Lora E, Payne M (2007) A política das políticas públicas: progresso econômico e social na América Latina: relatório 2006. Banco Interamericano de Desenvolvimento e David Rockefeller Center for Latin America Studies, Harvard University. Tradução: banco Interamericano de Desenvolvimento. Rio de Janeiro: Elsevier Washington, DC

Stone D, Patton B, Heen S (2004) Conversas difíceis, 8th edn. Elseiver, Rio de Janeiro

Ury W (2007) O poder do não positivo: como dizer não e ainda chegar ao sim. Elsevier, Rio de Janeiro

Vasconcelos CED (2008) Mediação de conflitos e práticas restaurativas. Modelos, processos, ética e aplicações. Editora Método, São Paulo

Warat LA (2004) Surfando na pororoca: o ofício do mediador, vol 3. Fundação Boiteux, Florianópolis

Weber M (1981) A ética protestante e o espírito do capitalismo. Pioneira/UnB, São Paulo

Weber M (1999) Economia e sociedade. Fundamentos da Socilogia Compreensiva. UNB, Brasília

Wolkmer AC (2001) Pluralismo jurídico. Fundamentos de uma nova cultura no direito, 3rd edn. Alfa Omega, São Paulo

Articles

Marra R (2005) Max Webber: razionalità formale e razionalità materiale del diritto. In: Sociologia del diritto. Rivista quadrimestrale fondata da Renato Treves. Università Degli Studi di Milano. Milano, XXXII/2–3

Reis E (1989) Política e políticas públicas na transição democrática. RBCS 9:3

Spengler FM (2021b) O pluralismo jurídico e os meios extraestatais de administrar conflitos. Novos Estudos Jurídicos (UNIVALI) 26:293–311

MIX
Papier aus verantwortungsvollen Quellen
Paper from responsible sources
FSC® C105338

If you have any concerns about our products,
you can contact us on
ProductSafety@springernature.com

In case Publisher is established outside the EU,
the EU authorized representative is:
Springer Nature Customer Service Center GmbH
Europaplatz 3, 69115 Heidelberg, Germany

Printed by Libri Plureos GmbH
in Hamburg, Germany